Education and Examination Systems in Ancient India

S. NARAIN

KALPAZ

ISBN: 978-93-5128-251-8 (HB)

First Published, 2017

Published by

Kalpaz Publications
C-30, Satyawati Nagar,
Delhi – 110052
E-mail: kalpaz@hotmail.com
Ph.: 9212142040

Printed at: G. Print Process, Delhi

Cataloging in Publication Data—DK
Courtesy: D.K. Agencies (P) Ltd. <docinfo@dkagencies.com>

Narain, S., author.
Education and examination systems in ancient India / S. Narain.
pages cm
Includes bibliographical references.

1. Education, Ancient—India. 2. Education—India—History. 3. Examinations—India—History. 4. Educational tests and measurements—India—History. I. Title.

LA36.N37 2016 DDC 370.954 23

Foreword note by Prof. G. Ram Reddy, Chairman, University Grant Commission on the book of the author 'Examinations in Ancient India'.

PHONE: 331 7143
GRAMS: UNIGRANTS
TELEX 316 5913
FAX: 331 5288

Professor G. Ram Reddy
CHAIRMAN

विश्वविद्यालय अनुदान आयोग
बहादुरशाह ज़फ़र मार्ग
नई दिल्ली - ११० ००२

UNIVERSITY GRANTS COMMISSION
BAHADURSHAH ZAFAR MARG
NEW DELHI-110 002

F O R E W O R D

I am pleased to write this foreword to Mr. S. Narain's book which I found to be very refreshing to read.

At a time when doubts are being expressed about the efficacy of of our examination system, an insight into the ancient examination system may serve an invaluable aid in evaluating the present system and its evolution from the beginning.

It is interesting to read the examination methods followed in ancient India to evaluate the knowledge of students as mentioned in the book. The basic ideals of ancient system some of which may still be relevant could be kept in view while attempting a scheme of examination reforms and providing a national reorientation to the system.

An extensive study to throw an adequate light on the ancient methods of Examinatiuon has perhaps been an unexplored area. Shri S. Narain's book on Examinations in Ancient India traces the system of examinations from it's faint beginning from the time of the Aryans to it's devecceloped state as reflected in Nalanda, Vikram Shilla Universities. I hope the book may be of interest to educationists, academicians, and to the students of history who are keen to have a deeper insight in the subject of educatiopn and examination.

G. Ram Reddy
(Prof. G. Ram Reddy)

PREFACE

What was the examination system in Ancient India? How evaluation of students for their performance in their studies was done? Were the great universities of ancient India like Nalanda, Takshilla etc attracting students even far in countries were awarding any degree of Diploma. Was any enterance test conducted by them? Very little is known to the people at large in this regard and hardly any academician or educationalist has shed adequate light on these points.

The book is therefore an attempt to bridge the gap of knowledge and provides a deeper insight in to the various kinds of test and different evaluation system followed in Ancient India besides the pattern of education.

At a time when India is poised to revise the existing examination system a peep into the Ancient system will be a worthwhile exercise as any scheme of reform should have its root in Indian soil.

S. Narain

CONTENTS

1

The Great Indian Heritage

1

THE GREAT INDIAN HERTIAGE

Indian is the heir of a civilization which is at once more ancient and alive than in any other country in the world and is largely the outcome of a well-nigh homogeneous pattern of myths and values, and a social order that it has evolved through fifty centuries of struggle, gradual assimilation and synthesis.[2] It has faced and often succumbed to many foreign invasions and submitted to foreign rule, but its social and cultural life has remained intact and, instead of being damaged or destroyed by these violent impacts, has been enriched and endowed with strength to develop and grow.

At the vast lithography ancient history many civilizations sprang up but have now most of them have become outlived as under :

EGYPTIAN CIVILIZATION

One of the oldest one, developed arond 7500 years ago and lasted about 5000 years.

Fig. 1 :

Under Egyption Civilization the sphinx at Giza is a mythological animal with the body of a lion and head of a man, It meant to gaurd the pyramids

MESOPOTAMIAN CIVILIZATION

In western Asia developed around 7000 years ago and continued up to 500 B.C.

GREEK CIVILIZATION

It continued till about 1400 B.C. followed by Mycenaean civilization in mainland Greece and continued till about 800 B.C.

ROMAN CIVILIZATION

It became one of the greatest civilizations evolved in Italy. It began to flourish after the sixth century B.C. and became outlived.

CHINESE CIVILIZATION

Emerged along the banks of the river HWANG HO under Shang dynasty during the period 1750-1100 B.C. and was succeeded by Chou dynasty ruling china from 1100-250 B.C.

It will be seen that many a civilizations emerged developed but almost all became out lived and perished. Indian civilization has the distinction of being still alive still vibrant and still continuing. Fire altars and fire sacrifice i.e. Hawanas and yajanas are being performed in large numbers. Rig Ved Hymns particular Gaytri mantras are being recited by Hindus with great reverence. The great epic of Ramayana, Bhagwad Geeta still adore with the shelf of homes of most of Hindus. Jainism, Buddhism emerged 2-3 B.C. are being practised in increasing numbers and so on.

Fig. 2 :
Performing Yajnas in Altas under Hindu Religious rituals is a common sight even today

The greatness of Indian Civilization lies in the fact that it has not hesitated to absorb whatever came in its way from other lands and other peoples in its long and chequered career. Thus, in the languages, in the religions, in the life, customs and traditions of the people, there has been a continuous flow and intake from outside. Whatever has come in its way has been absorbed and assimilated and has become part and parcel of its own inheritance. It has not remained as a mere adjunct or addition, but has become an unrecognizable part and parcel, a true accretion. This power of absorption and assimilation is as live and active today as it was ever before. The key to Indian life and development is to be found in a certain systematisation of manners, beliefs, and ethoes the balanced pursuit of the four-fold goals and because its ideals and concepts are universal in their application and not limited either territorially or by time or by any other limiting factor the indian civilization is an alive today as before ever.

REFERENCES

1. Hon'ble Dr. Rajendra Prasad, the First President of India, in his FOREWORD, note on 'Indian Heritage'.
2. Hindu Civilization - Dr. R.K. Mukherji.

2

Modern System vs Ancient India

2

MODERN SYSTEM VS ANCIENT INDIA

"Education must aid in self fulfilment and not in the acquisition of mere objective knowledge and not the amount of information that is put in our brain and runs roit."

– Swami Vivekanand

The word 'Examinations' for a student of modern edu cation causes panic & horror and while taking an examination he feels like a tiny boat in tempest, raised one

Fig.1

moment on the foamy crest of a billow of hope and dashed down into a yawning chasm of despair the next, rolling at the mercy of question paper of an examination being set at expected or unexpected lines, as the entire outcome of the education he has received, is the examination result.

The education system thrives on with main emphasis on examination result and the teachers relate their instructions from examination point of view neglecting the other important aspects of examination too subtle to be tested. The book market is flooded with 'guides', 'guess papers' and 'keys' containing ready made material for the examination to be swallowed by the students, the only objective being to score good marks and getting a diploma or a degree.

TYRANNY OF AN EXAMINATION

The mental phobia of failing in examination drive many students to kill themselves consuming poison or hanging by ropes. (A study conducted by a news magazine reveals that each year, some 4,000 odd students take their lives due to exam or failure fear). Says Aruna Broota, psychologist, Delhi University, "The rate of Board or University examination driven suicides is much higher than newspapers incidents reported."

Others who do not dare to kill themselves are full of stress and anxiety, having pressure of performance, and with burden of expectations making the modern day students' life very

Fig (2)

stressful. Over 80 percent of them report significant examination anxiety before their papers, resulting in the increase of emotional concerns including depression and immense worry about the future. Peer pressure, family expectations as well as the child's own perceptions about him/herself and what he/she wants to achieve all exacerbate the stress experienced.

On the basis of helpline calls from students & parents for the last several years, the following figure emerge-

FIGURES SPEAK

4,000 A study conducted by a news magazine reveals that each year, some 4000 odd students take their lives due to exam. or failure fear.

61% Students appearing for Boards suffered from anxiety, irritability, mood fluctuations fear.

60% felt isolated during preparatory holidays due to lack of interaction, strict regimen at home/this adds to stress.

50% Experienced cognitive problems-lack of concentration, difficulty in retention and recall of lessons.

62% of students appearing for Boards examination suffered from anxiety, irritability, mood fluctuations and fear.

40% felt isolated during preparatory holidays due to lack of interaction, strict regimen at home / this adds to stress

50% experienced cognitive problems- lack of concentration, difficulty in retention and recall of lessons.

The exams are fast loosing their trustworthiness on account of number of malpractices being indulged therein. Mass copying in examinations, replacement of answer books, mass boycott, late declaration of result are among few of the maladies besetting the present system of examination. Secrecy of question papers which is of cardinal importance in the present system, is violated blatantly with frequent instances of leakage of question paper.

CHEATING GOES HI-TECH

Cheating particularly copying in school & college examinations has assumed an alarming proportion, which is not limited to India but has become global phenomon. A survey conducted by an agency makes a sensational revelation. Accordingly the students to the extent of 25-30% themselves have admitted to have copied in the examination without being detected by the investigation personnel drafted for the purpose. In postgraduate & professional examinations High Tech devices are resorted to for cheating. Scanning of the question paper is done within minutes by a device installed in a pen which is smuggled out and answer of the questions thereafter reaches in scanned manner. With the advancement of technology even more sophisticated ingenious mechanism may be devised for cheating, thus, making a mockery of assessment system.

FAILURE OF SYSTEM

Is academic excellence a measure of achievement quotient? No. "Over the years in our society, success has come to have a very narrow definition. There is hardly any corelation between successful people and high percentage in Board/University exams. What really makes for a successful person today is drive, the ability to solve problems, communication skill, etc.

"Were the great personalities of India the Mahatma Gandhi and Pandit Jawahar Lal Nehru secured top positions in their terminal examinations." Ibrahim Lincon one of the most renowned president of USA has ever topped the examination? Newton who was

titled as 'Father of science' was he brilliant student? The answer is perhaps 'NO'. Unbelievable but true that the most eminent scientist of modern centuries Einstein and the famous mathematician of India i.e. Ramanujam failed in his civil examinations[1]. Lord Maynard Keynes, perhaps the most influential economist of the past half-century, received his lowest marks in economics. Note the irony that it is examinations, not the candidates, which actually failed and the number of unsung failures and injustices of the system are thousands of times greater than those which are well known.

Swami Vivekanand, a well known saint and thinker of India, exhorts the students of modern education, pointing out its aimlessness.[2]

"Getting by heart the thoughts of others and stuffing your brains with them and taking some university degrees you consider yourself educated. Is this the education? What is the goal of your education?" True, many students are totally ignorant of their goal of life and are like a rudderless ship, which sails on the waves of chance and does not know

its destination. Education must aid in self fulfilment and not in the acquisition of mere objective knowledge and not the amount of information that is put in our brain and runs right there.

The education being imparted in modern India with maladies afflicting to our students proceeding from educational objectives too narrowly conceived, merely passing examination and getting jobs, must assimilate the ideals of ancient Indian education system.

ANCIENT INDIA

On the contrary, the ancient Indian education was aimed at character building[3]. The true education seeks to train the mind as the instrument of knowledge to overhaul the mental apparatus itself. The aim of supreme education is to address itself to the principle of knowing, the root from which the knowledge springs and grows rather getting by heart a whole library.

There is an interesting reference in Chhand-Upanishada to amplify the universal truth. Where Narada 'a great rishi

---

3. स हि विद्यातस्तं जनयति।। सच्चेष्ठं जन्म।।
शरीरमेव मातापितरौ जनयतः।। शास्त्रैरधिगतानामिन्द्रिय दौर्बल्याद्
विप्रतिपन्नानां शास्ता निर्वेषमुपदिशेद् यथाकर्म यथोक्तम्।।
आपस्तम्ब ध.सू. 1।1।1।17; 1।5।10।12

approaches Sanat Kumara with a request to teach him. On being asked what he has already studied, Narada acknowledges[3]:

"Most reverend Sir, I have studied:

The Rig Veda, the Yajur Veda, the Sam Veda, the Atharva Veda and Ayur Veda, Itihasa—Purana, Grammar, and the Pitrya, the Arithmatic, the Davia, Astrology, Logic, the Deva Vidya. the Brahma Vidya, the Bhuta Vidya, the Military Science, the Sarpa and Deva Janan Vidya (the Science of Snakes and their Vemons), the science of making perfumes, dancing, singing, playing and other fine arts. All these I have studied Sir, but still I am in sorrow. Lead me thee over, I pray, to the further shore that lies beyond sorrow."

The supreme aim of education is summed up in the reply of Sanat Kumara to Narada.

"What you have studied is but words."[4]

This perfectly applies to modem education, which is by and large of informative kind.

Imagine the glimpse of ancient education system—Hermitage of a rishi is situated on the bank of a pious river far

4. Yajurveda (Taitti Sam. VI.3).

Fig. 3

from the madding crowd of urban life in a solitary place with high natural surrounding. At the break of dawn the entire forest is resounded with the recitation of text of scriptures by the students and sacred fire is burning in hearth. At the central place the acharya or guru is sitting with students around him in respectful manner. They are all observing strict Brahmacharya. A spirit of renunciation is pervading among them.

As per procedure of ancient education a student admitted by a Rishi or Acharya or preceptor under his studentship through Upanayana ceremony was required to undergo strict Bhramcharya and was known as Bhramchari and was expected to observe two-fold course of discipline, physical and spiritual, the later means worshipping, control of senses, practising austerities, etc. Every student used to get up early in the morning before sun rise.

With teacher's home as school, a student was considered as a part of family of Guru who constituted a constant stimulus to the ideal to which the Guru was dedicated. The student was to imbibe the inner spirit of life and mental faculty of his teacher being in constant and intimate association with him. The students were wholly dedicated to their teacher who was beholden as spiritual father giving a new birth[5] to them unfolding their intellectual and mental faculties.

There was no monetary consideration for imparting education.

It was the firm belief that a man owes three debts which must be repaid, one being Rishi debt owing to learning and acquiring knowledge. Spreading the knowledge and to distribute the fruits of knowledge to the people, to the society was the only way of repayment of the debt[6].

ALL ROUND DEVELOPMENT

The ancient education was not only for self realization or salvation of a man but was also having the orientation and traits of all round development, meaning spiritual, mental, moral and physical. The days and hours of study were very limited one and the remaining time was spent in extra-curricular activities. The pupil would perform yajna or fire sacrifice every morning with his guru. Even he would sweep the ground and attend menial services but the teacher would never utilize the labour of his pupil for his own selfish purpose. Every student would lead the life of strict discipline and complete control on his senses and serve his teacher day & night. In fact this all was aimed for the all round development and shaping a distinct personality.

PERFECT EQUALITY & SELF SUFFICIENCY

The students under the pupilage of a preceptor were treated alike. There was no discrimination between rich and poor and a perfect equality in every regard was observed. Shrimad Bhagwat Purana-a popular scripture of Hindus mentions the story of Lord Krishna and Sudama, the former was a prince and a later was the son of a poor Brahmin however the perceptor would treat them equally without making any regard of their financial and social or royal status.

One of the negative aspect of the modern education is that a student is always dependent upon his parents. He or she only gets mostly bookish knowledge, and not is exposed of the real conditions of life and daily house hold work i.e. preparing food, grow fruit plants, attending cleanliness of his house etc. A subject "Work Experience", introduced recently in school education does not serve the desired purpose. Also the parents have to support the child in matter of fees, dress etc. However, in ancient system a student was moulded for self-sufficiency. The school was a small integrated community self sufficient in every way. The students would tend cows, collect firewood and alms from householders, without putting any burden on their parents and after completion of his education every student was a self-sufficient personality, well trained to enter the life as householder after getting married.

COMPLETION OF STUDIES

The studentship was brought to an end after the completion of studies and was marked by a ceremony called 'Samvartan'.

As per the procedure of the ceremony, the student would take bath with flavored water. He was given a set of beautiful clothes to be put on by him. All the signs of Brahmcharya ie. girdle, kofin, begging bowl, would be removed and he was considered eligible to enter into the next stage of life. ie. Grahst Ashram. He was considered qualified to take part in debate.

The aforesaid Indian system has produced many a great men who made significant contribution to the world stock of educational thoughts. It possessed elements which were of great value and are still relevant.

India is experimenting with various schemes of educational and examination reforms and therefore the basic ideal of ancient system of education which is a national heritage may be kept in view to bear the best fruits of success and to preserve our own genius and individuality.

REFERENCES

1. वेदास्त्यागश्च यज्ञाश्च नियमाश्च तपासि च।
न विप्रदुष्ट भावस्य सिद्धिं गच्छतिकर्हिंचित्॥मनुः॥2197

2. सोऽहं भगवो मन्त्रविदेवस्मि, श्रुतं ह्येव में भगवद्दृशेभ्यस्तरंति शोकमात्मविदिति। सोऽहं भगवः शोचमि। तं मा भगवाञ्छोकस्य पारंतारयत्विति। तं होवाच-यद्वै किचैतदध्यगीष्ठा नामैवैतत्॥3॥
छान्दोग्योपनिषद् 7।1।3

3

Ancient Concept of Education & Examination

3

ANCIENT CONCEPT OF EDUCATION & EXAMINATION

"Eucation is no exotic in India. There is no country where the love of learning has so early an origin or has exercised so lasting and powerful an influence".

F.W. Thomas

The ancient views, thoughts and tendency are well re flected in the field of education than any where else. Learning in India through the ages had been prized and pursued not for its own sake, but has been sought as the means of salvation or self-realization, attain the highest end of life. Even the sight of a learned man was considered as holy.

Education was considered as the highest form of wealth which can neither be stolen by the thieves nor robbed of by the robbers. The highest importance attached to education is well evident from the fact that Manu the Hindu law givers exhort the parents without mincing words that the mother and father of a child depriving their kid education are no less than the enemy of their son. *"Mata shatru pita bari ye ne balo na pathitay".*

ANCIENT IDEOLOGY & PRINCIPLE :

Education must aid in character building and personality development and not in the acquisition of mere objective knowledge. It is more concerned with the subject than the object, the inner than outer world.

According to the ancients, individual is the chief concern and centre of education, Education also is necessary for individual and there shall be is an intimate relationship between the teacher and the pupil. The social psychology has proved that every individual has his own equipment of emotins, action-attitudes, and ways of thinking, which is the gift of the traditions and the social environment in which he is brought up. India has believed in the domestic system in both technical and general Education, and not in the mechanical methods of large

production in institutions and factories turning out standardized articles. The making of man depends on the human factor. It depends on individual attention and treatment to be given by the teacher. Here the personal touch, the living relationship between the pupil and teacher make education. The people belong to the teacher and not ot an institution or the abstraction called the school. Each scheme of training must, therefore, take into account the individuality of a person.

ANCIENT EXAMINATION SYSTEM

What was the evaluation system in Ancient India? Was there any examination held? Was there any ranking of students? How were the pupils assessed in term of their adequacy of knowledge?

The answer to these questions is shrouded in obscurity and rather mystery. The awareness and the knowledge on these points is far from being revealed by any academic personality or historian as the ancient Indian literature does not furnish any direct evidence on this subject. At best some isolated references are evinced in a casual manner. However, a thorough and extensive study and by tying bits of evidence some useful inferences can be drawn to conceive the picture of ancient eyaluation system.

CONCEPT OF AN EXAMINATION

An education system could be thought of comprising the following three processes:

(a) Teaching Process
(b) Learning Process
(c) Evaluation Process

Under the modern system the above three processes work almost independently and hardly any integration or synchronization exists. The students are taught by separate teachers for each subject of study as per time table framed by the institution and each of the teacher deals with his subject in his own manner as per contents of curriculum. As regards the learning process the student grasps the knowledge of the subject separately depending upon his attitude and calibre and does not learn the full quantum of knowledge of what has been taught to him, lie at best learns certain percentage of knowledge of the prescribed curriculum of study and imbibes the same through the examination which is conducted annually or biannually. If he has learnt and imbibed 60% of what has been prescribed to be taught, he is considered to be a 1st class student and if just half of the knowledge, he is an average boy and if less than half but not less than 1/3rd he is still certified as has passed the course of study/examination.

The contents which a student reproduces in an examination are evaluated by the examiners who are appointed separately for cach subject of study. In most of the cases they have not taught the subject to the students whom they are called upon to evaluate. They are not aware to what depth the teacher has gone. They carry out the evaluation works per their own without forming accurate conception of the teaching depth and learning attitude of students. This results into a very heterogenous situation and the evaluation done by them is bound to be erroneous. Also no integrated view of the knowledge of a student comprising together all the subjects of study is available. Under this system there are various fallacies as the student does not learn in full as to what he has been taught, does not imbibe the all, what he has learnt and he is not evaluated in full what he has imbibed. This defeats the very purpose of evaluation.

HOW WAS THE ANCIENT SYSTEM WORKING?

Under the ancient system, all these three processes i.e. teaching, learning and evaluation processes were perfectly integrated. The Acharya was the teacher as well as evaluator and was exercising full supervision over the students who were treated as his family members as residing with the teacher was one of the essential conditions of studentship. The teacher was fully aware what has been learnt by a student including the area of his weakness. Monitoring was done by the teacher daily[1] to ensure that the student has fully learnt the previous lesson given to him. As such, the gap between the teaching and learning was the minimum. An ideal of the perfect integration was envisaged through the *upanayana ceremony* which was performed for admitting a pupil into studentship, during which the teacher holding the student proclaimed:

"They heart shall dwell in my heart. My mind, thou shall follow with thy mind."[2]

No better compliments are possible to mark the total merger of the mental faculty of the student with that of the teacher bringing the gap between teaching and learning as zero. Evaluation of a student was a continuous process as examinations were a daily affair through monitoring. The mental calibre and the qualities of head and heart imbibed by a student together with strict discipline, observing other austerities, were open to the teacher. Therefore, his assessment regarding a pupil was the real one. He was totally free from any prejudice towards his pupil and would treat him as his son[3] and family member.

The completion of study of a student was marked by 'Samvartan' ceremony on being satisfied that the latter has gained requisite knowledge. The student was now termed as 'Snataka' and was presented to a learned Assembly' where occasionally some questions were put to him to adjudge the standard of knowledge of the student.

MODES OF EVALUATION

In corollary to the above system of evaluation as was being generally followed in ancient India, the extensive study of the old literature provides a glimpse that the under mentioned kinds of tests and mode of evaluation were followed by the ancients:

(i) Screening test for admission
(ii) Entrance test for higher education
(iii) Continuous assessment for grading of students
(iv) Terminal Examination.

Under the ancient system a student aspirant for Vedic knowledge had to approach a reputed Acharya for studentship and the Acharya with a view to adjudge the suitability and deservedness of the student for the education would ask certain questions and also the family background of the aspirant student before granting him studentship. There was no question of any fee or monetary consideration. The student had to undergo a kind of mental and moral test for admission to the course. This procedure formed an inseparable part of ancient Indian education right from the Vedic period. The screening was necessary to ensure that only the right type of stuff gots entry into Vedic schools[4(a)] and d astrous result might follow, if indiscriminate admission was granted to every student for Vedic education.

ENTRANCE TEST FOR HIGHER KNOWLEDGE

In Rigveda hymn[5] X-71.8, there is mention of learned assemblies called 'Brahman Sangha' where learned person met for discussion and disputation of the various points pertaining to Vedic knowledge of higher order. The entrance to these assemblies for the aspirant student was linked with satisfactory answering of questions put to the students. Similarly

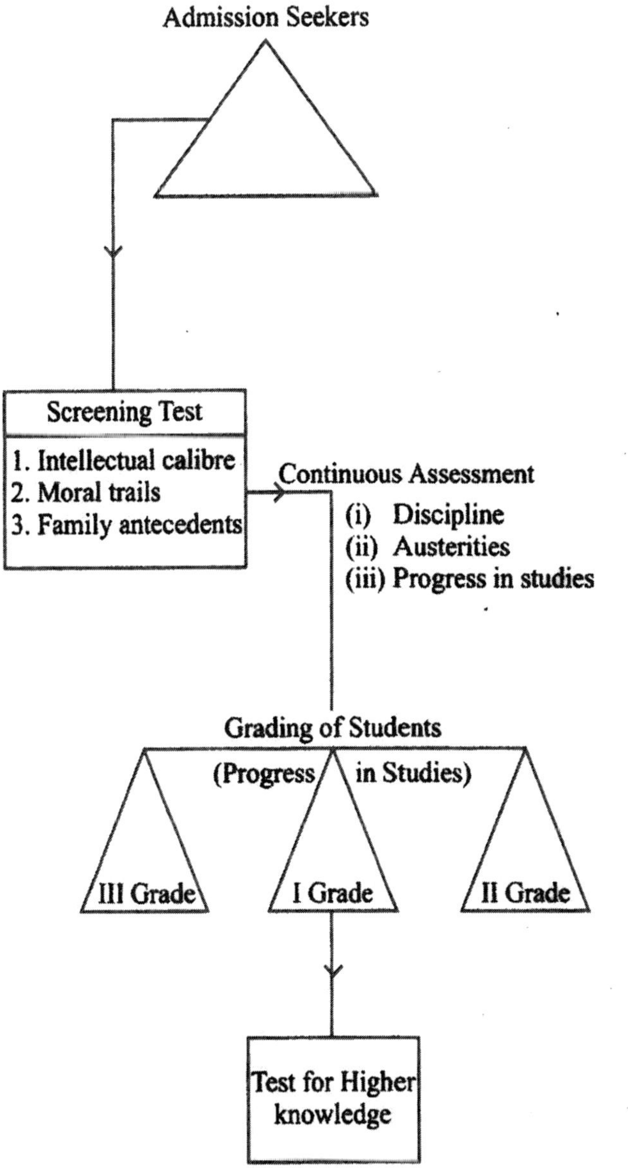

Examination and Evaluation Model of Ancient India

Upanishadas contain several references to the effect that higher knowledge (of philosophical doctrine) was imparted to the aspirant person after subjecting him to a kind of test of exacting moral standard. Nachiketa and Upakosala are the examples to uphold the point. In Nalanda University the entrance to the college of higher education was allowed after the students got through the oral test given by Dwar Pandita to adjudge the basic adequate knowledge of that student in which 7 out of 10 would fail.[6] This all shows that entrance test for higher education of knowledge has been one of the important characteristic features of ancient evaluation system.

CONTINUOUS ASSESSMENT FOR GRADING OF STUDENTS

The Rigveda hymn X-71Y[7] which has been explained by Yaska a famous commentator on Veda, mentions the three grades of students and those of higher grade were only allowed to pursue higher education, perhaps this is only possible as a result of close monitoring of students.

In fact, this was one of essential features of evaluation system of ancient India. There were daily exams and teachers would suspend the further teaching till the students have not learnt the previous lesson.[8] This clearly amounts to continuous assessment of students. It is on the basis of this system that the teacher would satisfy himself that his pupil had the requisite proficiency and knowledge and he was allowed to undergo 'Samvartan' ceremony to mark the completion of his studies.

TERMINAL EXAMINATION

Education in ancient India was characterised by high aims of character building, self fulfilment and shaping a distinct personality as brahmcharin, besides intellectual knowledge of Vedas and other sciences. Therefore, conducting terminal examination was no answer to evaluate the total attainment of a student and no system of conducting terminal examination for declaring a student successful or otherwise as in modern times was in vogue. However, there are evidences that some preceptors or Acharyas have invoked the method of evaluating their pupils in respect of their educational proficiency through a terminal examination. Panini the famous grammarian of ancient India was the pioneer to have introduced the system of terminal examination and the students were given different grades depending upon their performance in the test.[9] Similarly at Mithia University (700 AD).) 'Shalaka' system of terminal examination was followed. A page of text book pierce last by a needle driven through the pages of book was given to a student to explain it to the satisfaction of the teacher.

Besides the above the teacher at his discretion was free to give some imaginative type of test to any of his students to adjudge his knowledge. Zivaka a medical student of Taxila University is the example who was tested similarly by his teacher. However, there was no universal practice of testing the student's knowledge through conducting a terminal test.

EXTERNAL CHECK ON EVALUATION STANDARD

The Vedic schools run by Acharyas were fully autonomous in their functioning and the Acharya was the sole padcgogic authority. The snatakas produced in such schools must have attained proper standard and proficiency in their knowledge before their ceremonial completion of study and then to be called and looked upon as snataka. Therefore the system did contain certain inbuilt provision to exercise a check on the standard of evaluation and education. There was a tradition[10] and procedure that a snataka after having undergone 'Samvartan' ceremony was taken to a learned assembly by his Acharya and was introduced as such where occasionally some questions were asked. There are repeated references to this effect in ancient literature. Vasisht Dharm Sutra 3/23, Baudhyan Sutra 1-1-9 and Brih.Upanishada 6-2-1[11] furnish evidence on the point.

Obviously the answer given by the snataka would provide a glimpse of the standard of education he had received from the Acharya and also the evaluation of student in term of educational attainment. There is great philosophical value yoked to this tradition as the Acharya would agree to the saruvartan ceremony or bath ceremony' far the student after the latter had finished his study to the satisfaction of the teacher and had gained requisite proficiency in knowledge.

REFRENCES.

1. Mil. Panh. I.P. 18.
2. Sankhayana Srauta Sutra 'ii' 4.1
   Asvalayana Srauta Sutra i. 21.7.
3. पुत्रमिवैनमभिकांक्षन॥ आप. ध.सू. 1।2।8।24
4. आश्रमस्थास्त्रयों मुख्याः परिषत् स्याद् दशवराः।
   वसिष्ठ ध.सू. 3।23

4(a) Manu Smriti II-114-115.

5. हृदा तष्टेषु मनसो जनेषु यद्वाह्यमा संयजते सरवाय
   अत्राह त्वं वि जहुर्वेद्याभिरोहृब्रह्मणो वि
   चरंत्यू त्वे (Rig Veda 10.71.8)
6. Hiuen T siang (Beal's translation vol. 'II' 102)
7. अक्षण्वंत कर्णवंत सखायो मनोजवेष्वसमाबभूवः।
   आदध्नास उपकक्षास उ त्वे हृदा इवस्नात्वा।
   उ.त्वे. ददृश्रे॥ (10.71.7 Rig Veda)
8. अप्रतिभायां यावन्तं काल न वेद तावन्तं कालं तदधीयीत।
   विपरीतोच्चारण रूपं स्खलित मेकं जातं सः।
   सि. कौमदी प्र. 320
9. ऐकन्यिकः यस्याध्ययने प्रवृत्तस्य परीक्षा काले
   विपरीतोच्चारण रूपं स्खलित मेकं जातं सः।
   सि. कौमदी प्र. 320
10. चातुर्वैद्यं विकल्पी च अङ्गविद्रसंपाठकः।
   आश्रमस्यास्त्रयो विप्राःपर्षदषा दशावरा॥ बौधायन ध.सू.1।1।1
   वृह. उप. 3।3।1: 3।6।4

11. वेत्थ यथेमाः प्रजाः प्रयत्यो विप्रतिपद्यन्ता3 इति? नेति होवाच। वेत्थो यथेमं लोकं पुनरापद्यन्ता3 इति। नेति हैवोवाच। वेत्थो यथाऽसौ लोकं एवं बहुमिः पुनः पुनः प्रयद्रिर्न संपूर्यता3 इति? नेति हैवावाच। वेत्थो यतिथ्यामाहुत्यां हुतायामापः पुरूषवाचो भूत्वा समुत्थाय वदन्ती3 इति? नेति हैवोवाच। वेत्थो देवयानस्य वा व पथः प्रतिपंद पितृयाणस्य वा यत्कृत्वा देवयानं वा पन्थानं प्रतिपद्यन्ते पितृयाणं वा। आप हि न ऋपेर्वचः श्रुतम्।

द्वे सृती अश्रृणवं पितृणामहं देवानामुत मर्त्यानां,
ताभ्यामिंद विश्वमेजत्समेति यदन्तरा पितरं मातरं चेति।
नाहमत् एकं चन वेदेति होवाच॥2॥

(Birth, Upanishada) 6.2-1

3A

Grading System of Evaluation

3A

GRADING SYSTEM OF EVALUATION

Under the current system of evaluation, students are given terminal examination of 2-3 hours for every subject of the course and at the end of the year or semester his output in the form of answers written by him during the small period of 2-3 hours is assessed in terms of marks assigned by the examiner. The system is certainly fallacious for several reasons. Firstly the three hour output of the student should not be treated as the true index of the total knowledge attained by him in the whole year. Secondly the assessment by the examiner is always subjective and may differ from examiner to examiner. If the same answering script is sent to another examiner the marks given would differ. A research study in this regard has revealed variation upto 20%, as such the system assigning marks in numerical terms is erroneous.

On the contrary under the ancient system of evaluation neither there was any terminal examination nor assessment in term of numerical marks. Infact Education in Ancient India was characterized by high aims of character building, self fulfilment and shaping a distinct personality, besides intellectual knowledge of Vedas and other sciences. Therefore, conducting terminal examination was no answer to evaluate the total attainment of a student and no system of conducting terminal examination for declaring a student successful or otherwise as in modern times was in vogue.

CONTINUOUS ASSESSMENT

The entire course of Vedic study was not of continues type stretching to a long term twelve years but was a graduated one divided into several parts which may be termed as modules in modern terminology. Each of such modules was to commence with a Vrata. The duration of these Vrata extended to even full year or so. The teacher would carefully watch the progress of students and his inner capacity by Vratas and also his academic performance. The main Vatas to be observed by students have been mentioned as under:

1. *Savitra Vrata :* This refers to the introduction of Savitri Verse to the student.

2. *Sukriya Vrata :* This refers to the commencement of the study of the main versa to the student.

3. *Anuvachana :* Which means the way in which Vedas are to be studied.

4. *Sakvara : Vritika, etc :* They refer to the study of Aranyaka and Upanishada Brahamna,etc.

The above Vratas suggest that unless the teacher is convinced about the satisfactory completion of study of one module, the commencement of the next module would not ensue. The assessment of the teacher in this regard was final and total.

GRADING OF STUDENTS

The Examining bodies now-a-days are awarding grades to the students on the basis of one or two terminal examinations. The sutra works provide evidence that the students completing the course of study, who were called 'Snatakas' were also placed into three grades. The normal period of studentship was prescribed as twelve years on completion of which a student was supposed to bathe as per the ceremony of 'Samavartana' and was called snataka. Therefore, he would enter 'Grihistha Ashrama'- the second stage of life and ceases to a Brahmachari. There are three categories of Snatkas mentioned under Gobhila:

1. Vidya Snataka
2. Vrata Snataka
3. Vidya Vrata Snataka

VIDYA SNATAKAS

Those who complete their study of Veda and bathe before the normal period of studentship.

VRATA SNATAKAS

Those were just the reverse kind who bathe before completing their study but they have completed the normal period of studentship.

VIDYA VRATA SNATAKAS

Those who complete the prescribed period of Brahm acharya and also their study.

This suggests the three grades of students:

1. Intellectually brilliant students complete their whole study before the lapse of the period of studentship i.e. twelve years and are called Vidya Snatakas.
2. Medium students from intellectual point of view finish their study just in twelve years and are called Vidya Vrata Snatakas.
3. Below average students who fail to complete their study obviously give up a part prescribed period of twelve years. Such students obviously give up a part of their study though they are also Snatakas but are called Vrata Snatakas.

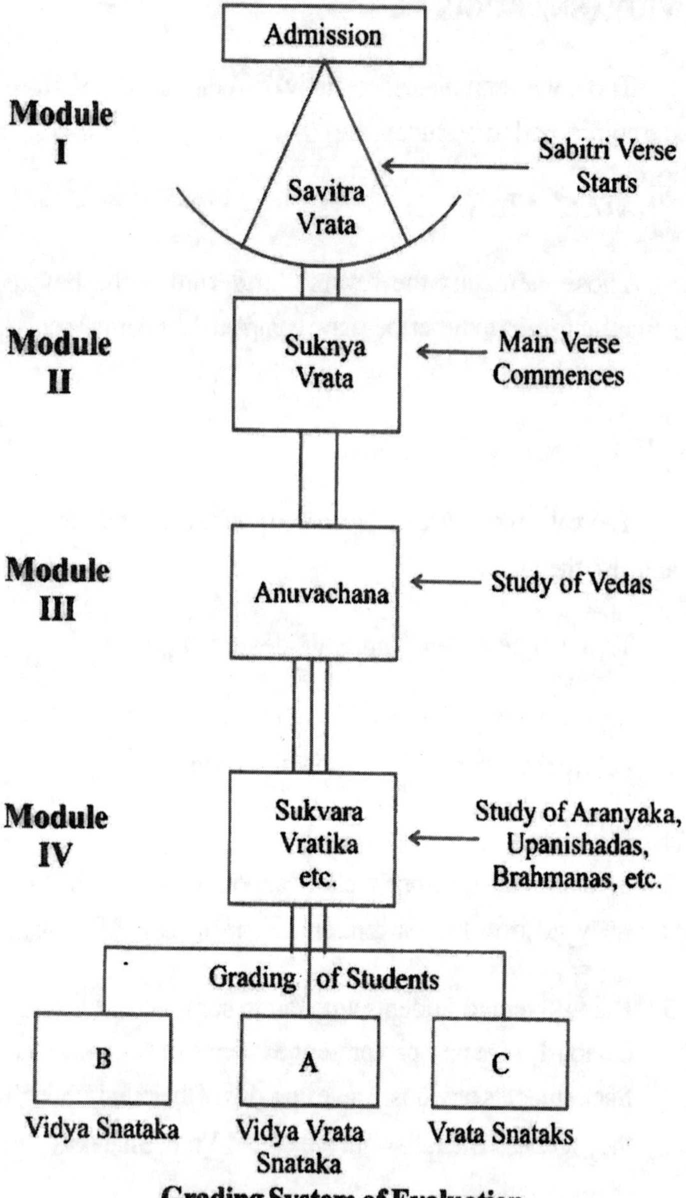

Grading System of Evaluation

This is exactly similar to modern grade system under which a 'Board of Examinations' does not declare a student pass or failed but he is given a grade. It is interesting to infer from the above that under the ancient system whatever finished was finished thoroughly to the satisfaction of teacher and the student was having complete knowledge of that which has been covered by him. However, under the modern system a student acquires a certain percentage of knowledge of the whole course but not the complete knowledge of any subject.

GRADING OF STUDENTS IN VEDIC PERIOD

It has been mentioned in Rig Veda that students who have studied the same shastra may possess equal senses like eyes and ears but may be just like tanks of varying depth. 'Sayana' a famous commentator on Veda has inferred that the students were given three grades as under:

1. Students of high ability were placed in *Ma/ia Prazanam grade.*

2. Students of medium ability were given *Mad/I yama Prazanan grade.*

3. Student of low ability were given *Alpa Prazanan grade.*

These grades were given to the students as a result of their continuous assessment by their teacher. The system can be well compared to that followed by various examining bodies now-a-days on the basic of pedagogical research. Students placed in the highest grade i.e. Maha Prazanan were only allowed to pursue the highest knowledge. While those of Madhyam Prajanan grade i.e. medium ability were expected to be settled in their occupation i.e. ploughing, loom etc. However pupil evaluated as low ability students i.e. Alpa Prajanan grade were to be weeded out i.e. dismissed from studentship. This is further corroborated from 'Nirukta i. I'. Infact continuous assessment and grading of students has been one of essential features of evaluation system of ancient India. There were daily exams and teachers would suspend the further teaching till the students have not learnt the previous lesson. This clearly amounts to continuous assessment of students. It is on the basis of this system that the teacher would satisfy himself that his pupil had the requisite proficiency & knowledge and he was allowed to undergo 'Samvartan' ceremony to mark the completion of his studies.

REFERENCES

1. अप्रतिभायां यावान्तं कालं न वेद तावन्तं कालं तदधीयीत। यदा जानापादुषतो यजुष्ट सामत इति॥61

- बौधायन ध.सू. 11916

4

Vedic Period Education & Examination System

4

VEDIC PERIOD

EDUCATION & EXAMINATION SYSTEM

The Ancient Indian education system is one of the oldest of the world civilization and has survived even after the repeated assaults and outrages made to destroy it from time to time. The system is followed even today in many old Pathshalas and Gurukulas existing in man towns and cities. Varanasi holds an important place in this regard. The glimpses of some of the important aspects of ancient Indian education e.g. observing Brahmacharya and pious relation between the teacher and the taught can still be seen in these Pathshalas, though the methodology and the curriculum of teaching have undergone a vast change.

The ancient Indian education has, passed through the following distinct spells[1]:

1. Vedic period (Prehistoric period to 1000 B.C.)
2. The epic period (between 1000 B.C. and 800 B.C.)
3. Period of Upanishadas (800 B.C. to 500 B.C.)
4. Period of Dharm Sutras (600 B.C. to 200 B.C.)
5. Buddhist period

It may be mentioned that neither any border line can be drawn to mark the duration of a period nor any precise division is possible. In fact there have been various streams of education surfaced from time to time in ancient India. In most of the above cases also more than one streams were going on simultaneously. It is the dominance of literature and the institutions belonging to a stream influencing the masses governing the naming of a period or stream. It is also possible that besides the above, some more streams would have appeared but since these could not wield any appreciable influence among the masses and failed to make any dent, therefore, dried down soon.

EXAMINATIONS

As regards the evaluation of students in respect of their educational attainment during these periods, various methods were invoked by preceptors, acharyas who were autonomous in their functioning, to suit the conditions of the age, the contents, curriculum and aim of education. However, the basic ideal that the education should be imparted[2] only to those who possess appropriate moral and mental aptitude for the kind of education, was not sacrificed. Also the teacher would continue to be the sole padegogic authority to decide whether the student had completed his study.[3]

THE VEDIC PERIOD

Vedic period is the most ancient period marking the dawn and meridian of Aryan civilization when the Aryans mostly got settled in small villages surrounded by forests. In fact the origin of Hindu civilization lies in forests rather than the metropolitan cities or towns, as Rabindranath Tagore has rightly pointed out:

"Here in India, the forest not the town is the fountain head of a its civilization."

"It is the forest that has nurtured the two great ancient ages of India, the Vedic and the Buddhist."

Vedas which are considered very sacred literature of Hinduism and are the oldest literary work, (especially the Rigveda) have a very important place in the history of world civilization. The hymns of Vedas are still looked upon as revealed words of God. In fact the entire culture and religion of Hindu civilization have been evolved on the be rock of these Vedas.

The word 'Veda' generally means knowledge from the root *Vid* i.e. to know and refers to the collection or compilation of sacred knowledge or supreme knowledge.

RIG VEDA

Out of the four Vedas, Rig Veda is considered as the most ancient of all scriptures and gives an idea of the sublime doctrine and fountain of the Hindu civilization building up through ages. It is the compilation and collection of 1017 hymns divided into 14 mandals. According to Mocdonall and Bookyield, the composition and compilation of these hymns must have taken hundreds of years and centuries must have elapsed between the composition of the earliest hymn and the Sanhita of Rig Veda.

Sam Veda, Yajurveda and Atharva Veda

While the Rig Veda is the most ancient and most original work of Hindu civilization, the other Vedas i.e. the Sam Veda, the Yajur Veda and the Atharva Veda are the later compilation. In case of Sam Veda many of the verses have been taken from Rig Veda and the text is treated as collection of special melodies. In other words it gives the complete text of the songs for Soma rituals. The Yajur Veda contains the prayers and mantras and the sacrificial rituals which the priest has to perform. The other part of Yajur Veda consists of mantras in verses and in prose giving the sacrificial rites. It also prescribes the religious scheme and ordering the Hindu life in the course of ceremonies and the sacrifices to be performed at different occasions. The Atharva Veda comprises of prescription of herbs as remedy against diseases like fever, jaundice, etc.

EDUCATION IN RIG VEDA

The education in Vedic times therefore, comprised of learning these hymns by recitation of sacred text which was cultivated as an art itself. The text of Veda was to be learnt by the method of hearing it from the lips of the teacher. Writing of Veda as an aid to memory and education was not allowed and was considered as sacrilege. The Vedic education was, however, not confined to merely recitation with correct pronunciation, the contemplation and comprehending the meaning of hymns was more important. Learning without understanding has been condemned repeatedly.[4]

'He is only the bearer of a burden, the block head who having studied the Veda does not understand its meaning'.

Grasping and understanding the meaning of sacred text was a very difficult and prolonged process, where thinking, meditation and concentration was utmost necessary together with stiff discipline sustained by a life of austerities, tapas and yoga and then only realization of truth was possible.

In Vedic period the education system was working on the basis o some standardized and well established ideals and practices. There were domestic schools run by Rishis[5] or teachers admitting pupil in small number. The studentship started with a ceremony called Upanayana" by the chosen teacher. Before granting studentship, the Acharya, the teacher would satisfy himself regarding- the suitability of the pupil being imparted education. It was believed that through the Upanayan ceremony the teacher would hold his pupil within him to impart him a new birth—and the pupil would emerge as *Divija* (twice born). He would be a reborn one as changed person both externally and internally. Now the student would be called Brahmachari or Vratachari and would live with his teacher under prescribed discipline and regulation which comprised of wearing Kusa Girdla and deer skin, collecting and tending fuel and worshipping, firm control of senses and practice of austerity. Dedication to his Acharya was most important.

In the time of Rig Veda the education was imparted into two stages. At primary stage the pupil were given recitation and memorizing of text resounding like croaking of frogs after rain. The second stage which was the advanced one comprised of tapa and yoga. Every pupil had to undergo concentrated contemplation and depending upon their mental and spritual capacity, their dedication and sincerity, variation was noticed among them. They were compared like tanks of varying depth. Those of average calibre were sent to engage themselves in different occupations i.e. agriculture, ploughing, carpentry, etc. while those in the higher grade in terms of their spiritual and mental aptitude were only sent for higher learning. The students found unfit to undergo tapa and yoga exercises were weeded out. In the time of other Vedas i.e. after the period of Rig Veda, the higher education was meant for learning priesthood and ritualistic religion.

HIGHER EDUCATION IN VEDIC PERIOD

The higher education was not meant for all. Only those belonging to higher grade i.e. *Mahaprajanan* and were eager for quest of higher truth and supreme knowledge and also were able to undertake concentrated contemplation were allowed to pursue the same. They were also required to undergo meditation and tapa to seek truth. However, during the period of Sam Veda, Yajur Veda i.e. later Rig Vedic period, the higher education began to centre more and more in ceremonial and sacrificial rituals. The subjects of higher education were the elaborate details and procedure of various sacrificial ceremonies and mechanical aspects of worship.

A sacrificial ceremony comprised of three functions to be performed by priests. The leading priest was called Hotri and recital of the hymns in the honour of the God of worship was done by him during the course of sacrifice while the priest reciting hymns in honour of Soma' who was also regarded as God and was worshipped normally on every such ceremony was called 'Udgatri'. The actual ritual was performed by and large by other priest called 'Adhvaryu'. Each priest was supposed to be well versed in all these functions and the higher education comprised of training the students to perform any of these rituals. However, in the later time, there were separate priests for each of these orders and separate schools were functioning for each of them. Thus, there were schools for imparting education for Udgatri, Adhvaryu and Hotri Priests and these were related to Sam Veda, Yajur Veda and Rig Veda respectively.

EVALUATION SYSTEM IN VEDIC PERIOD

System to be followed in a particular age or period of history has a definite co-relation with the mode and kind of education being imparted in those days. In Vedic period the education comprising of text of Vedas to be recited orally with particular phonography followed by meditation aiming at seeking of truth, evaluation through conducting a single or terminal examination would have no meaning. Also there is no direct reference available to spell out the methodology followed by the Acharyas to judge the adequancy of knowledge of his pupil. However, from the study of various Hymns and Stanzas some inference could be taken out as under:

MORAL TEST FOR GRANTING STUDENTSHIP

The common practice being followed in those days for granting studentship was that the aspirant lad would approach his chosen Acharya or Rishi with fire wood in his hand and oral prayer for initiating him. The Acharya would ask his name and put to him some questions to adjudge his moral standard and sincerity and suitability of receive Vedic Education.

The following citation quoted from Nirukta furnishes an idea about the guidelines to be followed by the Acharya for granting studentship to a student.

"The Goddess of learning approached Brahmna saying 'protect me; I am thy treasure. Do not expound me to the following unworthy persons—him who is jealous, who is wanting in simplicity and straight forwardness or who is devoid of self control.'

This has also been put in sutras by 'Manu' in his work "Manu Samriti."

This suggests that a Acharya while agreeing to the granting of studentship must enquire about the antecedents of the student and through casting his searching look on the boy and putting some relevant searching questions would satisfy himself about the suitability of the pupil on the ground of moral fitness for being granted studentship. This was the simplest form of aptitude test or entrance test for admission. The studentship commenced by initiating the student through a ceremony called Upanayana which lasted 3 days at the end of which the student was reckoned as Brahmachari as already mentioned.

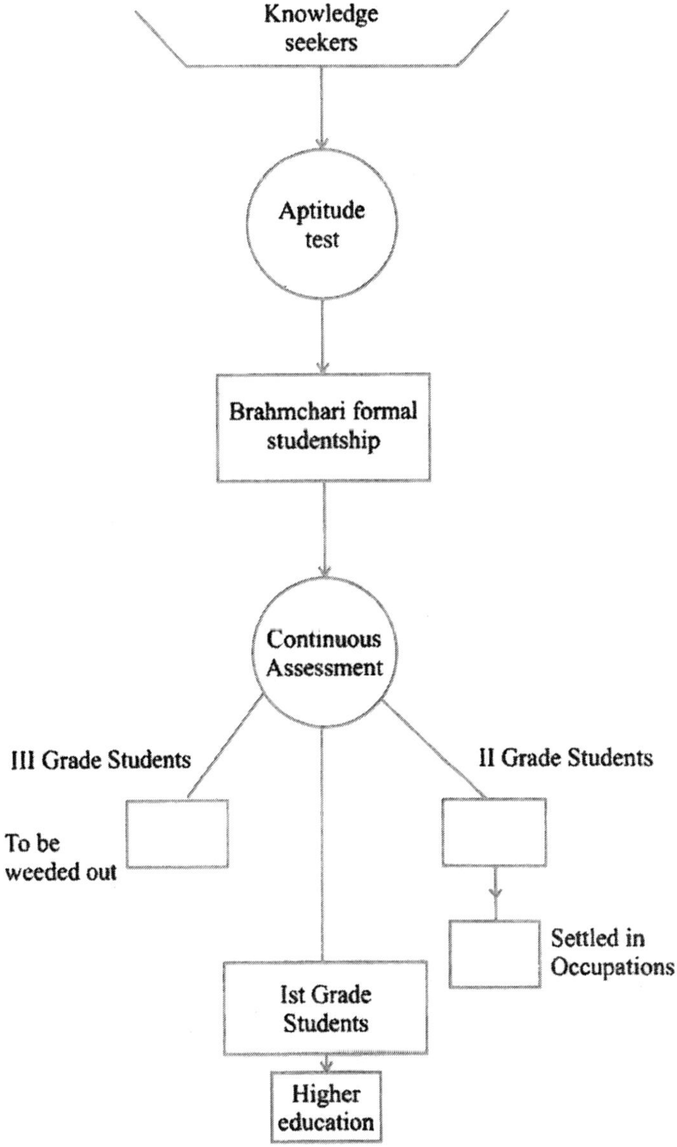

Evaluation System in Vedic Period

CONTINUOUS ASSESSMENT

After having been granted the formal studentship or taking to Brahmacharya, it was compulsory for the student to live with the teacher. This was the most essential aspect of Vedic Education. There appears to be a system of continuous assessment and evaluation as transpires from the guidelines contained in an old text quoted in 'Nirukta' which reads:

"The teacher must avoid teaching isolated syllable and he should teach only such a regular pupil as well as one who is especially qualified by his intelligence or asceticism or thirst for knowledge."

In an another old text, the discipline of Brahmacharya has been statec one of the essential conditions for continuation in studentship. This also suggests that a pupil who does not observe his duties was liable to be expelled.

GRADES OF STUDENTS

It has been mentioned in Rig Veda[7] that students who have studied the same shastra may possess equal senses like eyes and ears but may be just like tanks of varying depth. 'Sayana' a famous commentator on Veda has inferred that the students were given three grades as under:

1. Students of high ability were placed in *Ma/ia Prazanan grade.*

2. Students of medium ability were given *Madhyama Prazanan grade.*
3. Student of low ability were given *Alpa Prazanan grade.*

These grades were given to the students as a result of their continuous assessment by their teacher. The system can be well compared to that followed by various examining bodies now-a-days on the basis of paedegogical research. Students placed in the highest grade i.e. Maha Prazanan were only allowed to pursue the higher knowledge. While those of Madhyam Prajanan grade i.e. medium ability were expected to be settled in their occupations i.e. ploughing, loom etc. However pupil evaluated as low ability students i.e. Alpa Prajanan grade were to be weeded out i.e. dismissed from studentship. This is further corroborated from 'Nirukta i. I'

ENTRANCE TEST FOR LEARNED ASSEMBLIES

There were learned gatherings of highest order where the learned Brahmans and the students of higher knowledge used to get together. This transpires from Rig Veda[8]. These assemblies were also called 'Brahmana Sanghas'. They were meant for advancement of knowledge and diffusion of learning through discussion where each one was supposed to be possessed of adequate knowledge to qualify himself for gaining entrance. It is obvious that fellowship of such academies was not open to every one who cannot contribute a bit there—in and they were excluded from the gathering.

The admission to these assemblies was made after testing the knowledge of young participant through putting oral question of searching nature to qualify for participation in learned gatherings.[8]

EARLIEST FORM OF TEST

The above constitutes the earliest form of test under the ancient Indian system of Education and perhaps the world padegogy. This compares favourably with that was followed in the middle ages in Europe later on[9].

VOCATIONAL EDUCATION IN VEDIC PERIOD

The Vedic period was not the age of saints and seers alone. In fact the Vedic education was limited to few only. Hymns of Rig Veda provide a glimpse of the various crafts and vocations as were being pursued in those days. It is on account of its progress in various crafts, cottage type industries and agriculture laying a strong foundation of economic development that India was reckoned for its wealth and riches. There are several references in Rig Veda suggesting that a sizeable population of society was engaged in various crafts and vocations.

A part of Rig Veda hymn reads as under

"I am a poet, my father is a physician and my mother grinder of corn."[10]

This shows the diversive economic pursuits as were being followed by the members of a family.

Agriculture was the favourite vocation of ancients and that necessitated ploughing by bulls tied with leather strings, irrigation wells for supplying water to fields by a chain of buckets driven by stone pulley etc. Surely occupations like cattle rearing, black-smithy, leather tannery, carpentry for making ploughs, door windows, oars and chariots were in progress. Practising medicine was one of the noble profession. A considerable part of Atharva Veda is devoted to the treatment of different ailments like, fever, leprosy, jaundice etc. The science of Architecture was also in developing stage. Description of one hundred stone cities and forts confirms it.

There must have been a system of imparting vocational and industrial training turning out the craftsmen and technicians in various trades as described in a separate chapter of the book.

REFERENCES

1. **See Ancient Indian Education**
   By F.E. Keay, pp.: 14, 18, 21 and 27
   Professor Robert Phillip Gold man, University of California, Reference Hindustan Times, dated 15 Aug. 1992.
   Ancient Indian History and Civilization ***By Majumdar***

2. कृत्वाऽनुशातस्य वा स्नातम्। गौतम ध.सू. 2।56
3. विद्या ब्राह्मणामेत्याह् शेवधिष्टेऽस्मि रक्षमाम्।
असूयकाय मां मादास्तथा स्यां, वीर्यवन्तमा॥ मनुस्मृतिः 11-114
यमेव तु शुचिं विद्यात्रियब्रह्मचारिणाम्।
तस्मै मां बूहि विप्राय निधिपायाऽमादिने। म.सम्. 11-115
4. **Nirukta-i-18 by Yaska**
5. **Yaska and Durgacharya- the two commentators define 'Rishi' as the person who is possessed of vision, to whom practising austerities, the Vedas revealed their meaning without their study by him.**
6. आचार्य उपनयमानो कृणुमे गर्भमन्तः।
तं रात्रीस्तिस्त्र उदरे विभर्ति द्रण्टुमभियंन्ति देवाः॥
अर्थर्ववेद 11।5।3
6. (a) ब्रह्मचारी चरति वेविषद्विषः स देवानां भवत्येकमङ्गम्
तेन जायाभन्नविदंदृह्स्पतिः सोमेन नीतां।
जुह्वं न देवाः 10.109.5 ऋग्वेद
7. अक्षणवंत कर्णवंत सखायो. मनोजवेष्वसमाबभूदुः।
आदध्नास उपकक्षास उ त्वे ह्रदा इव स्नात्व॥
8. ह्रदा तष्टेषु मनसो जनेषु यद्ब्राह्ममा संयंजते सरवायः
अत्राह त्वं वि जहुवद्याभिरोहब्रह्माणो वि।
चरंत्यु त्वे (ऋग्वेद 10-71.8)
9. **Ancient Indian Education F.E. Keay p.14.**
10. पूर्वामनु प्रदिरां याति चेकितत्सं
रश्मिभिर्यवते दर्शतो द्रयो दैव्यो दर्शतो रथः।
अग्मन्नुवथामि पौस्येन्द्रं जैत्राय हर्षयन्
वज्रश्व यद्भवयो अनपच्युता समत्स्वनुपच्यता॥
- ऋग्वेद 9.112.3

5

Later Vedic Period

5

LATER VEDIC PERIOD

In the whole world there is no study, except that of the originals, so beneficial and so devoting as that of the Ouphuekhat (Upnishadas). "It has been the solace of my life, it will be the solace of my death".

- Sehopen, a great Philosopher.
(on reading of Upnishadas)

PERIOD OF UPANISHADAS (800 B.C. to 500 B.C.)

This is the period when Indian education evinced a rare intellectual attainment and when highest quality of philosophical thoughts emerged out, which have no parallel even today. The message of Upanishadas is still awakening the world, unfolding the physical mysteries and human speculation regarding some of the ultimate problems of life. The period of Upanishadas' is considered between 800 B.C. to 500 B.C.

The Rigveda discusses two clear streams of religious thoughts. The original stream of pure thought was that enunuciated by Rishis—the direct seers of truth and is marked by meditation, contemplation and *'tapas'*. However, the second stream comprises of sacrificial rituals and priesthood. By the end of Vedic period the second stream became dominated and religion was bogged down by ceremonial sacrifices with its details more and more elaborated. The following kind of literature emerges out the two streams:

(i) Brahmanas

These are the massive texts in prose and their subject matter is practical directions for performance of Yajana for sacrifice.

It is the literature of priesthood. At the end of Brahmanas are certain treaty known as 'Aryanka' or forest book i.e. to be studied in forest by the sages.

(ii) Upanishadas

Deals with philosophical speculations and all the vehicle of metaphysical and mystical truth. The number of Upanishadas is as large as two hundreds. However, the oldest Upanishadas-chhandogya and *Brihadaranyaka* considered to be the oldest are supposed to belong to 600 B.C.

The Upanishadas give evidence of a rare intellectual attainment and significant contribution of philosophical thoughts to the world. An impressed and overwhelmed Sehopen - a great philosopher, by the reading of a translation of Upanishada, made the following compliments:

"From every sentence deep original and sublime thoughts arise and the whole is pervaded by a high and holy and earnest spirit. Indian air surrounds us and original thoughts of kindred spirits. And oh, how thoroughly is the mind here washes clean of all early engrafted Jeurish Superstitions and of all Philosophy thaf cringes before these superstitions. In the whole world there is no study, except that of the originals, so beneficial and so devoting as that of the Ouphnekhat (Upanishadas)."

"It has been the solace of my life, it will be the solace of my death."

THEME AND MESSAGE OF UPANISHADAS

1. Upanishadas speak of the knowledge which is the foundation of all arts and sciences i.e. supreme knowledge after knowing of which nothing remains to be known and this has been termed as 'Para Vidya' which means the knowledge through which the ultimate reality is known. All other kinds of knowledge i.e. Vedas, Vedangas grammar phonetic, etc. and other subjects of study are included under Apara Vidya and even after mastering all of these, one still feels some insufficiency, some inadequacy till he learns Para Vidya.[+1]

2. The conception of Ashramas took its birth from Upanishadas which later on formed the bed rock of Hindu way of life. According to which the whole life span of an individual has been divided in the four stages:

(i) Brahmcharya Ashrama

It is the period of studentship and discipline to give necessary knowledge and training to enable a person to lead happy and balanced life.

(ii) Grihstha Ashrama

This is the second stage of life which means life of house holder to do wordly duties.

(iii) Vanprastha Ashrama

After having brought up family one should retreat and should lead life of forest hermit.

(iv) Sanyas Ashrama

It is the period of renunciation and to free oneself from attachment to the world.

The conception of ashrama appears to have taken birth assuming the total span of life of hundred years. In fact in Vedas, there are hymns[2] praying for hundred years of life and this total period was later on divided into four parts with a duration of 25 years each.

SYSTEM OF EDUCATION

The tradition evolved in Vedic period for imparting education were by and large continued in Brahmna Upanishada period also. The admission into studentship was granted through

Upanayna Ceremony. The common procedure or system has been that the aspiring pupil would approach the teacher with firewood in his hand and this was the indication that the student desires to study and is willing to submit himself to the strict discipline of Brahmacharya and he is willing to serve the teacher and to maintain sacrificial fire. Before initiating him into studentship, normally, the teacher would ask about his name and the family he belonged. The ceremony of initiation lasted 3 days and comprised of putting brahmacharya dress by the student, a girdle of Kusa grass, skin of black deer, long hairs observing certain Vrata, prayers, etc. The pupil was supposed to emerge as divija i.e. twice born thereby, which was considered as the spiritual birth, more pious to first birth[3]—the physical birth, which he owed to his parents.

The normal period of studentship was twelve years. Sometimes a student having been initiated into pupil-age was not given Vedic learning for years together to the discretion of the teacher? Instances of longer period of studentship are also available. For Brahman youth[5] it was not the universal custom to enter upon the life of studentship. However, once having entered upon brahamacharya the pupil would have to abide by the strict discipline comprising of prescribed regulations and rules in that regard. The student had to live in the house of his teacher and the external duties incumbent upon him were tending fire, tending cattles, guarding the house of his teacher and to go about begging. As regards the study, the student would start with the knowledge of the pronunciation, little knowledge of phonology and elementary grammar etc.

METHOD OF TEACHING

A unique method of teaching as discernible from the study of Upanishadas was based upon discussion in the form of questions and answers between the teacher and the taught with explanations supported by stories, parables and illustrations. The pupil would ask questions which were followed by explanations and discourse by the teacher freely utilizing stories and parables. Usually broad hints were furnished by the teacher to be worked out by student himself through 'Manna' means introspection and contemplation by the pupil.

SUBJECTS OF STUDY

During the period of Upanishadas the curriculum of study was quite exhaustive which included much more than the knowledge of the Vedas. There is a beautiful reference which furnishes a good idea about the subjects of study.

'When Narada approached Sanatkumaras with the request to teach him, Sanatkumaras asked him:

"Please tell me (first) what you know, thereafter, I shall tell you what is beyond", Narada said I have studied, most reverend Sir' the Rigveda, the Yajurveda, the Samveda, as the fourth, the Atharveda, as the fifth the Itihasa—purana (the Bharata); the Veda of the Vedas (Grammar); the Pitrya (the rules for the sacrifices for the ancestors); the Rasi (the science of numbers); the Daica

(the science of portents); the Nidhi (the science of time); the Vakevakya (Logic); the Ekayana (ethics); the Devavidya (etymology); the Brahmavidya (pronunciation, siksha, ceremonial, kalpa, prosody, chhandas); the Bhutavidya (thc science of demons); the Kashatravidya (the science of weapons); the Nakshatra Vidya (Astronomy); the Sarpa and Devajana-vidya (the science of serpents or poisons, and the sciences of the genii. such as the making of perfumes, dancing, singing, playing, and other fine arts)."

EDUCATIONAL INSTITUTIONS

During the period of Brahmna Upanishadas three types of educational institutions were functioning:

1. *Domestic School*

Under the normal system of education prevailing in those days. a teacher would admit students of tender age at his own settled home to give instructions. When a student wished to become pupil of a teacher of his choice the recognised way of making request to him was to approach him with fuel in his hand. The admission of student was formally made through the ceremony of Upanayana or initiation as per ceremonial procedure prescribed for the purpose. The normal period of studentship was 12 years and only on permission, the student would leave for home after taking a ceremonial bath followed by the prescribed ceremony called 'Samvartan' and was considered as having completed the study.

2. *Mobile Debates*

The student who wished to pursue advanced study with the quest of further knowledge would travel far and wide with a view to receive instructions from celebrated teachers or to improve their knowledge through mutual discussion with other wandering scholars as there was a system in those days that advanced scholars would wander through the country in quest of knowledge and philosophical discussions were held in mobile debates where the knowledge gained in Vedic schools would get mature through discussion and friction of minds. These could also be termed as debating circles.

3. *Conferences*

Assemblage or congregations were sometimes convened by the kings where in rishis, thinkers and learned men throughout the length and breadth of the country were invited to exchange their views and to discuss philosophical issues. These could be well compared to thc conferences being held in modern times.

ASSESSMENT AND EVALUATION OF STUDENTS

As per normal procedure followed in those days a student aspirant for admission would approach the teacher running the school with firewood in his hands which amounted to application for admission in modern sense, He would say "I have come for Brahmacharya[8] (Studentship)." He thereby makes himself over to the Brahman (Teacher) who asks the name of the student and takes his right hand with himself and encloses the student from both sides with embrace reciting hymns and initiate the student as his pupil. The manner of asking the name and family antecedents was very casual and indulgent which suggests that the admission of students was made without any moral test and assessment. In fact, there are references where a desire and anxiety on the part of a teacher to attract more pupils is reflected. A passage from Taittarya Aryanka where a teacher prays for getting increasing number of students reads as: "O God may Brahmcharies come to me from all quarters"[9].

(i) *Assessment for Imparting Education*

The normal period of studentship was twelve years. However, a pupil having been granted studentship and initiated through Upanayna Ceremony was some time not imparted education (Philosophical doctrine) till the teacher has fully assessed him to be satisfied that the student is worthy to be imparted instructions. Satya-Kama Jabala* is one such example. He spent much more than twelve years as a pupil of his preceptor during which 400 cows became 1000 but he was imparted education only after he got through the test given by his teacher to return to the latter for instructions after the 400 lean and weak cows are tended appropriately to grow into 1000 healthy cows.

Similarly, Upakosla Kamalanayna who tended fire of his preceptor for twelve years was not found worthy to be imparted education though he was granted studentship and was initiated through Upanayana Ceremony. Such instances were, however, not common.

(ii) *External Test*

A student on completing his education and designated as Snataka was entitled to take part in debates and was some time put to a real test when he was confronted with questions put to him in a learned assembly or outside and his recognition as a scholar or a real snataka was linked with his satisfactory answering the questions failing which the student would return to his teacher or would go to another learned scholar for further instructions to make good the deficiency of knowledge.

The following evidences prove the contention:

(a) Svatketu Aruneya, a Brahman youth when he returned to his father after completing 12 years of studentship having studied all the Vedas—conceited and considering himself well read and *stem,* his father asked him: *"Svetketu, my dear, as you are so conceited, considering yourself well read and so stern, have you ever asked for the instructions by which we hear what cannot be pursued, by which we know what cannot be known"*[10].

On being expressed his ignorance the father himself undertook his study and imparted further education to his son at his home.

(*b*) Svetketu after completing his education and while sitting in a meeting of Panchala Parishad—an academy of scholars, failed to answer the question raised by the King Prabahana, went back to his father who was his teacher to point out the deficiency of education imparted by the latter and received further education from the king.

TEST FOR HIGHER KNOWLEDGE

A student aspirant for admission to higher knowledge was subjected to an exacting moral and mental test to prove his fitness to receive instruction to the satisfaction of the teacher. One of the most important component of test was being true quest for knowledge, then sincerity and proper mental calibre to imbibe the supreme knowledge. Numerous typical methods were followed to judge the above merit. Sometimes, a temptation was offered in lieu of higher knowledge, long waiting before giving instruction was also resorted to. Instances are available to bear out this fact.

Chhand-Upanishada IV-2 mentions a king's name Janasruti Pantrayana who approached Raikua for instruction and offered him 600 cows, a necklace and a carriage of mules in lieu thereof. However, the latter rejected the offer. Similarly Upakosala Kamalayana tended fire of Satya Kama Jabala for a period of 12 years[11] but found unfit for the higher knowledge, the latter did not agree to impart instruction. A beautiful case, as to how the sincerest desire of an aspirant student was judged by the preceptor for the supreme knowledge has been mentioned in Katha Upanishada[12] when Nachiketa approached Yama with the request of supreme instruction. Yama offered him a heap of wordly possessions namely gold, elephants, horses, Sons and grand sons even the monarchship of earth. However Nachiketa not the least tempted by the wordily pleasures replied: "*Keep thou thy horses......... No one can be made happy by wealth and Yama had to yield.*"

SNATAKA — GRADUATE IN MODERN TERM

Graduates passing out a degree course from a University now-a-days are called 'Snatakas'. In olden days 'snataka' would refer to the student who had taken bath (Samvartan)— a ceremony marked on completion of study of a student admitted to a school. The student was given bath by his teacher after the latter had satisfied himself that the pupil has completed his studies and he is now fit to go home from the point of view of his educational attainment.

As per the procedure of the ceremony, the student would take bath with flavoured water. He was given a set of beautiful clothes to be put on by him. All the signs of Brahmcharya i.e. girdle, kofin, begging bowl, would be removed and he was considered eligible to enter into the next stage of life i.e. Grahst Ashrama. He was also considered qualified to take part in debate.

NO DEGREES, NO DIPLOMA

A student having completed his studies and taken a ceremonial bath was not awarded any degree or certificate as the practice prevailing now. He was supposed to keep his knowledge fresh all the time and on his lips and would have to prove his educational attainment at any occasion i.e. debate or in other learned circle.

CONVOCATION ADDRESS

In fact no convocations as being held today to award degree or diploma to the students were held in ancient India. However, a student after completion of his study and leaving his 'Alma mater' was given the admonition address as under by his teacher:

"Say what is true! Do thy duty! Do not neglect the study of the Vedas. After having brought to thy teacher his proper reward do not cut off the thread of thy race. Do not neglect the sacrificial rituals due to the gods and fathers. Let your mother be to you like a goddess. Let your father be to you like a God. Let your teacher be to you like a God. Whatever actions are blameless those should be regarded not others whatever good works have been performed by us, those should be observed by you not others."[13]

What more beautiful valedictory address there could be to a student, entering into house holder's life.

REFERENCES

1. **Ancient Indian Education**

   by F.E. Keay, P. 18

   तस्मै स होवाच्च द्वे विद्ये वेदितव्ये इति ह स्म यद् ब्रह्मविदो वदन्ति, परा चैवापरा च॥4॥ **(Mundko upanishada 1-A-5)**

2. शतं जीव शरदो वर्धमानः शतं हेमन्ताञ्छतमु वसन्तानू।
   शतमिन्द्राग्नि सविता बृहस्पतिः शतायुषा हविषेमं पुनर्दुः॥
   ऋग्. 10।161।4; अथर्व. 3।11।4

3. आचार्य उपनयमानो ब्रह्मचारिणां कृणुते गर्भमन्तः।
   तं रात्रीस्तिस्त्र उदरे विभर्ति तं जातं द्रष्टुमभिसंयन्ति देवाः॥
   अथर्व. 11।5।3

4. उपकोसलो ह वै कामलायनः सत्यकामे जाबाले ब्रह्मचर्यमुवास। तस्य ह द्वादशवर्षाण्यग्नीन् परिचचार। स ह स्मान्यानन्तेवासिनः समावर्तयंस्तं ह समैव न समावर्तयति ॥1॥
   (छन्दो. उपनिषद 4.10.1)

5. **Chhand Upanishada, VI.I.I.**

6. **Narada has been mentioned as seer or Rishi in Atharva Veda and a pupil of Sanat Kumara in Cnhand Upanishada. In Puranas Narada has been described to have free access to all the Hindu gods being possessed of super natural powers.**

7. स होवाचरर्वेदं भगवोऽद्योमि, यजुर्वेदं, समावेवमाथर्वणं चतुर्थम्, इतिहासपुराणं पञ्चमं, वेदानां वेदं, पित्र्यं, राशि, दैवं, निधिं, वाकोवाक्यमेकायनं, देवविद्यां, ब्रह्मविद्यां, भूतविद्यां, नक्षत्रविद्यां सर्वदेवजनविद्याम एतद्भगवोऽध्येमि ॥२॥
   (छन्दो. उप. 7.1.1-2)

8. गौतममेत्योवाचं ब्रह्मचर्यं भगवति वत्स्याम्युपेयां। भगवन्तमिति। तं होवाच किंगोत्रो नु सौम्यासीति।

9. यथाऽऽव: प्रवता यन्ति, यथा अहं, एवं मां ब्रह्मचरिण:, धातरायन्तु सर्वत: स्वाहा। प्रतिवेशोऽसि प्र मा भाहि, प्र मा पद्यस्व ॥४॥

छन्दो. उप. *iv-4 (3-4)*

* *Satya-Kama Jabala*

As mentioned in Chhand, Upanishad Satya-Kama was the the son of a slave girl named Jabala and had no gotra or family name and of unknown father. Aspiring to become a Brahmchari to acquire knowledge he approached Gautama Haridru Makka for the purpose. On being asked regarding his family antecedents by the teacher, Satya-Kama repo0rted him the full facts and hid truthfulness impressed the Acharya who agreed to admit Jabala in his studentship exclaining:

"No one but only a Brahmana could speak out the truth like this. I shall initiate you." Satya-Kama was assigned the duty to tend the four hundred lean and weak cows of his Guru and he lived for several years in forest till four hundred cows grew into one thousand cows and on return the Acharya imparted him instructions. Satya-Kama later on grew to be a famous teacher and also established the school of Yajurveda.

10. Chhand. Upanishada, VI. 1,2,3.

11. उपकोसलो ह वै कामलायन: सत्यकामे जाबाले ब्रह्मचर्यमुवास। तस्य ह द्वादशवर्षाण्यग्नीन् परिचचार। स ह स्मान्यानन्तेवासिन:

समावर्तयंस्तं ह स्मैव न समावर्तयति॥१॥ (छन्दोग्य उप)
शतायुप: पुत्रपौत्रान् वृणीष्व बहून् पशून् हस्तिहरण्यमश्वान्।
भूमेर्महदायतनं वृणीष्व स्वयं च जीव शरदो यावदिच्छसि ॥२३॥
सन्यसे वरं वृणीष्व वित्तं चिरंजीविकां च।
कामानां त्वा काम भाजं करोमि॥24॥ (कठ.उप)

12. वेदमनूच्याचार्योऽन्तेवासिनमनुशास्ति। सत्यं वद। धर्मं चर। स्वाध्यायान्मा प्रमद। आचार्यय प्रियं धनमाहृत्य प्रजातन्तुं मा व्यच्छेत्सी:। सत्यान्नप्रमदितव्यम्। धर्मान्न प्रमदितव्यम्। कुशलान्न प्रमदितव्यम्। भूत्यै न प्रमदितव्यम्। मातृदेवो भव। पितृदेवो भव। आचार्यदवो भव। अतिथिदेवो भव। यान्यनवद्यानि कर्माणि तानि सेवितव्यानि न इतराणि। यान्यस्माकं सुचरितानि तानि त्वयोपास्यानि नो इतराणि। ये के चास्मच्छ्रेयांसो ब्राह्मण: तेषां त्वयाऽसनेन प्रश्वसितत्यम्। श्रद्धया देयम्। संविदा देयम्।

13. धिया देयम्। ह्रिया देयम्। भिया देयम्। संविदा देयम्। अथ यदि ते कर्म विचिकित्सा वा वृत्त-बिचिकित्सा वा स्यात् ये तत्र ब्राह्मणा: संमर्शिन: युक्ता आयुक्ता: अलूक्षा धर्म्मकामा: स्यु: यथा ते तत्र वर्तेरन् तथा तत्र यतथा:। अथाभ्याख्यातेषु ये तत्र ब्राह्मणा: संमर्शिन: युक्ता आयुक्ता: यतथा धर्म्मकामा: स्यु:, यथा ते तत्र वर्तेरन् तथा तेषु वर्तेथा:। एष आदेश:। एष उपदेश:। एषा वेदोपनिषत्। एतदनुशासनम्। एवमुपासितव्यम्। एषमु चैतदुपास्यम्। (तैत्तिरीय उप. १।११)

6

Period of Dharm Sutras

6

PERIOD OF DHARM SUTRAS

This period marked by a galaxy of preceptors like Manu, Panini, Gautam, etc. whose thoughts and ideas continue to be a veritable mine of information on the numerous topics of Human interest down to the present day. This is also called the period of Sutra literature. Here the preceptors summed up the entire substance of religion in the form of sutras. During Brahamna-Upanishada period there was a growth of vast and varied literature, the knowledge of which became more and more unintelligible as such there was a need of simplified literature and clear guidance and directions to be imparted in simple language and sutra literature was the result of that necessity. The period of dharmsutras is between 300 B.C. to 600 B.C. Their work namely Manu Smriti' and 'Ashtadhyayi' are still considered to be very authoritative and pioneer in contents. Kautilay's 'Artha Shastra' is also the work of this age. They other literature of this period comprises of Dharamasutras, Grahasutras, Upvedas and Vedengas like Sikshsa, Chhandas, Vyakarna, Nirukta, Kalpa, Jyotisha, etc compiled by various preceptors.

On going through the varied literature especially the sutras and smrities, one can have an idea of the educational system available in those times. The various ceremonies involved during the course of education are also mentioned therein.

However, the strict regulations framed by these preceptors gave rise to rigid caste system, so much so that only three twice born castes were declared eligible for education.[1] Elaborate, cumbersome rituals were prescribed to begin with, to continue with and to complete the study. Even days, timings, places and periods of study were fixed.

Receding were the days of Upanishadas where a king proclaims, "In my kingdom there is no thief, no miser, no drunkard, no man without altar in the house and no ignorant person.[2]

EXAMINATIONS

This period can rightly boast the credit to give to the world a form of terminal examination for the first time containing all the elements of an examination system and this is traced in the shlokas of Panini. The details of which are given in the latter part of the chapter.

EDUCATIONAL INSTITUTIONS

Vedic Schools Run by Acharyas

The normal type of educational institutions in those days were the domestic schools run by the learned Acharyas[3]. The teachers, wherein the students were admitted according to the discretion of these teachers took special care to see that the aspiring pupil has the right aptitude and the moral fitness for the kind of education i.e. Vedic education to imparted to him. Neither any monetary consideration nor any fee was expected from the pupil to grant studentship and to impart education The progress shown by the student and his conduct and sincerity to undergo strict disciplinary rules and the austerity were the factors governing the continuation of studentship under the Acharaya. The number of students admitted by the Acharyas were also comparatively smaller as the teaching was individual and the teacher had to attend each student separately. The capacity of the teacher's house accommodate students, was also an important consideration for putting a limit to the number of students for admission in the school.

Why Domestic System?

The ancient system of education insisting on the residence of the pupil in the home of his teacher was necessary to meet the demand of the educational method i.e. oral method which was followed in those days as a vast quantity of scriptures were required to be memorized with absolute accuracy and accent and pronunciation. As such personal and continuous contact between the student and the teacher was necessary. It was the first and foremost condition to reside with the teacher as his family member.

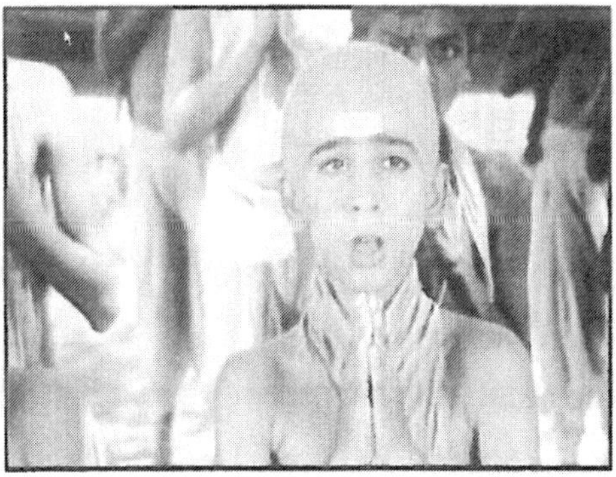

COACHING SCHOOLS RUN BY UPADHYAYAS

These institutions were to cater the need of supplementary instructions in Vedangas or a part of Vedas. These schools were conducted by upadhayas and the students admitted were given lessons in a particular subject on payment of fees[4].

DECISION-TAKING INSTITUTIONS

'Parishads' as existing in those days were not meant to impart instruction in a subject to the admitted students but to give decision which would be binding on the community. In fact it was an academy of experts for authoritative interpretation of a point concerning to Veda or largely on general conduct. Such institutions or parishads were existing in every educational colony or settlement. The composition of a Parishad would usually consist of ten members as under according to Manu[5]:

(i) Three persons each should know one of the three Vedas.
(ii) One logician.
(iii) One Mimansaka.
(iv) One learned man of Nirukta.
(v) Three men belonging to first three orders i.e. Brahmacharya, Grihastika, Vanprastha.
(vi) One who recites the institute of sacred law.

However, the constitution given by the other preceptors is slightly in variance with that given by Manu.

SCHOOLS FOR SPECIALIZED DISCIPLINES[6]

Evidence is not lacking in 'Sutra' works that not only the common Vedic schools with usual curriculum imparting education in Vedas and Vedic texts, etc. were functioning but separate schools for specialized disciplines or Vedangas' were conducted by learned 'Rishies' for studies" in:

(i) 'Vayakarana'
(ii) Jyotisha
(iii) General law – based upon religion or the discipline.

Panini's Vyakarna and his another work 'Ashtadhyayi' are the living examples of such schools. Similarly schools of Jyotisha undertaking the special study of the discipline must have come into formation. This view is further corroborated by the fact that we hardly know of any grammatical or anthrological work belonging to any of the Vedic Schools. Similarly in the case of development of Jyotisha which started as an anga of Veda, the famous work on Astronomy like Gargi Snahita' is not the product of any Vedic school and the cultivation of special school can only be the result of its phenomenal development.

Special law schools were also being run by preceptors and Rishies. The original Dharamsutras containing the moral duties and detailed rules were the subject of study of these schools including the law of partition and inheritance. The school run by under the name of 'Yaja Valkya' producing manuals and secondary smrities are the examples of such institutions.

EDUCATIONAL SYSTEM

The educational system as was being followed during Vedic and Upanishada period comprising of Upanayana ceremony for initiating the pupil for imparting education, thereafter, observing Brahmacharaya with strict rules, discipline and austerity, forsaking all worldly charms' and living with his teacher till the studentship ends, continued as usual. However, the system was perfected, details and rules of the system were codified, legislations were laid for observance and rigid regulations were framed for study and Brahmacharya, etc.

The main aim of education in this period was inter creational oriented to character building rather than the intellectual development. The routine of a student after his initiation through 'Upnayana' ceremony was set as per strict rules with no relaxation. It has been again and again emphasised that study of Veda without observing any austerity for self imposed restraints and discipline is infructicious.[7(a)] In Manu Smriti, in fact, mere intellect without moral training has been condemned at various places.

Introduction to Education

A child was introduced to education comprising of learning of Alphabet at the age of five by performing a ceremony called 'Tensur or Vidyarambha'. The occasion was marked by performing worship to 'Hari', Lakshmi and Sarswati and family vidya. The period from birth to 5th year was considered as the time to play.[7(b)] The ceremony performed was supposed to provide sacrement to the child according to Manu.

COMMENCEMENT OF' FORMAL EDUCATION

The beginning of Vedic education was marked by a ceremony called Upnayana' for which the pupil would approach the teacher of his choice and the latter after satisfying himself regarding the fitness and deservedness of the boy, would grant studentship. The formal enrolment and initiation was done through performing the cercmony of 'Upanayna' by the teachcr - the preceptor.

UPANAYNA CEREMONY

The normal age for Upanayna is prescribed as 8, 11 and 12 years respectively for Brahmna, Kshatriya and Vaisa by Manu. Yajavalyka and Apstamba also mention the same[8]. The views of other preceptors vary slightly in this regard. The maximum age limit has also been fixed as 16, 22 and 24 for these castes. The underlying idea for fixing the age limit has been as explained by 'Janmini' that a pupil elder in years will find Vedic study rather difficult and in the absence of strict discipline through brahmacharya, the mind may wander to extraneous distractions. The consideration of prescribing different ages appears to be I.Q. and aptitude for learning, and also the aim in life after study; though the point has not been clearly brought out by any of preceptors in his sutras.

UPANAYNNA CEREMONY COMPRISED OF AS UNDER

The young scholar after the preceptor has indicated his willingness to admit him for studentship was offered special dress and equipment of Brahmaehari consisting of skin of certain animals as upper garment and vasa the lower garment made of cotton clothes and other materials he was also given staff of wood and mekhala i.e. girdle of different materials. A Yagopavita—sacred cord was also to be worn by him in three sets of three threads each. The hair were dressed with a special arrangement. The student now properly dressed as *Brahmachari* was to pronounce the following:

"I have come here to be student, initiate me". The occasion was marked by prayer to gods for strength, mastery of all the Vedas, fame and bliss. A special prayer for intelligence was also offered. The Braiiamchari is now made to stand on stone symbolising strength and firmness. The teacher formally admits the students with the following words:

"Thy heart shall dwell in my heart. My mind, thou shalt follow with thy mind".

The Savitrivarta then begins lasting three days during which the student lives on special food. A rite called 'Medhajanana' is performed to invoke gods to enhance the mental power of the student.

A great importance has been laid to the ceremony of Upanayana, through which the teacher initiates the pupil to the studentship. The Upanayana does not only bring about a purifying influence on the student but he is supposed to accomplish a second birth[9] superior to man's natural birth as he is reborn by education and is called Divjareborn. No better compliment is possible to stress upon the importance of education by ancients. As per Manu, the Acharya through imparting the knowledge of Veda, builds the mind and soul of man. The birth which the teacher procures for the student is exempt from age and death.

SELECTION AND ADMISSION OF STUDENTS

The sutras made it incumbent upon the teacher to take great care to select the students for study of Vedas. It was considered disastrous to impart knowledge to the undeserved ones. A key note address by Manu reads:

"Let a Vedic preceptor should die with knowledge than impart into an unworthy recipient."[10]

As per system prevailing in those days an aspirant student would approach the teacher with a request to grant him studentship. It was the sole discretion of teacher to accept or reject his request, if, one is not considered fit to be imparted instruction on the basis of one's character, capacity and heredity.

CURRICULUM OF STUDY

The course of study prescribed for a student of Vedic school was quite comprehensive. As per Manu, the course included the following:

1. Three Vedas[A]
2. Vedangas i.e. Siksha, Kalpa, Grammer (Vyakarma), Nirukta and Chhanda[B]
3. Atharva Veda[C]
4. Upanishadas and Aryankas[D]
5. Puranas and Itiahas

The elaborate course meant for study well justifies the long period of studentship which may be as long as 48 years, if, a student wishes to study all the 4 Vedas. However, in any case he is supposed to learn by heart at least one Veda.

RULES AND REGULATIONS OF STUDENTSHIP

A student once admitted as Brabmachari by his preceptor for imparting education was expected to comply with the definite rules and regulations, of studentship.

Firstly, the student should stay in the house of his preceptor through out the period of studentship. The strict rule on the point was that a student must be in his teacher's house after the sun sets and before thc sun rises.

Secondly, a student after having been initiated must perform the fire sacrifice daily in the morning and evening till the time of completion of studentship and, therefore, he was supposed to coflect the fuel from forests.

Begging alms for himself and for his teacher was considered essential for a student. Then there were regulations governing student's life which briefly mention

1. Early rising[11]
2. Regular Prayer
3. Daily bath

4. Dress as prescribed
5. Staff
6. Sleeping on bare ground
7. Celibacy
8. Serving the teacher by word, mind and deed
9. Mental and moral discipline

THE PERIOD OF STUDENTSHIP

The length of the period of studentship was normally 12 years. In a passage Manu says, 'a twice born one shall reside in the residence of his Preceptor for the first quarter of his life. It is obvious that one could not determine the length of the period of just one quarter of his life. This suggests that the period could vary according to the aptitude of thc pupil. A clarification has been furnished in this regard in 'Apastamba' which mentions that a student after initiation shall reside for 48 years, if, he learns all the Vedas or least by half i.e. 24 years, if, two Vedas are studied, and 12 years if, only one Veda is studied, however, the shortest time, should be 12 years[2].

ACADEMIC SESSION

This means the number of days of teaching actually carried out in a Vedic School in a year. The session starts on the full moon of the month of 'Sravan[13] with the performance of a ceremony called Upkarman[14]. The session then continues till the full moon of the month of Posha and formally closes with Utsarjana ceremony. The total length of the session was 5 months in a year. During this period the private study of student was permitted as per regulations. The student was allowed self study of the Veda during the last nights of each month while in die dark nights vasanada comprising of grammar, astronomy, etc. were studied by the students.

METHOD OF TEACHING

For the purpose of teaching the student would keep ready in the morning rather in the last watch of the night. Self controlled, attentive, he will sit down to the right of the teacher with the permission of the latter. He shall do the achamana facing east or north and will embrace the feet of his preceptor, not only at the commencement of study but at the end of his lesson also. The teacher shall address him as 'O, you read now' and the pupil after purifying his body by three pranayamns shall utter the word Om[14] -before the actual instructions begin. The method of teaching was the oral one. This has been explained in Sankhyana, Grahasutra as under :

Firstly the text of a hymn of the Veda is taught to the student indicating the rishi, deity and meter of the hymn. Thereafter the teacher would go on reciting the hymn belonging to each rishi.

The reading lesson was followed by instruction and explanation. Maxmullar in his book 'History of Ancient Sanskrit Literature' furnishes some account on the method of teaching of Vedic text: 'The Guru himself takes his seat either on the east or to the north east. If, he has one or two pupil they sit at his right hand. If more, they sit according to the available space in the room and then each of them embraces the feet of his teacher and, say 'Sir read'. The teacher reciting the syllable begins with a Prashan' (question) and pronounces all the words with high accent and repeats certain words twice so that no word escapes the attention of his pupil. Whenever, difficult case of Sandhi occurs the Guru examines his audience and explains the dificulties."

CONFERRING 'SNATAKA' TITLE

The ceremony marking the conferment of Snataka title to a pupil is called 'Samavartana'[15] ceremony. It means close of studentship. The ceremony consists of removing of all external marks of Brahmcharya i.e. girdle, staff, skins, Brahmacharya robe, shaving the head and beard and bathing the student with perfume sandal wood powder and giving him new garments, ear rings, etc. and offering prayer by him. The student is now called 'Snataka'- a graduate in modern sense that who has bathed and this amounts to conferment of degree. The teacher then takes the Snataka to a learned assembly.

TEACHER'S HONORARIUM-GURU-DAKSHINA

Before a student takes final bath to be designated as 'Snataka' and before his studies are formally brought to an end, he should as a getsure of gratefulness give a present to his preceptor according to his capacity which may be field, a cow, a horse and even vegetables or any thing procured in righteous manner. The idea is to give pleasure to his preceptor and to express his gratefulness for the education given and sacred vow fulfilled. This is called Guru Dakshina.

APASTANBHA MENTIONS :-

The student shall procure in a righteous manner the fee for teaching of the Veda to be given to his teacher according to his power." However, any kind of remuneration can hardly discharge the debt of the teacher to the pupil and Guru Dakshina is only a gesture to express that student will be ever indebted to the teacher for the education given, vow fulfilled and first of the ashramas of life completed.

Manu says'[6]

"When the student is about to take final bath let him procure a present for the venerable man according to his ability, viz., a field, gold, coin, a cow, a horse, a parasel and wheat, grain even vegetables, etc., and thus give pleasure to his teacher."

EXAMINATIONS IN SUTRA PERIOD

The Sutra works provide some evidence as to the nature of certain tests and evaluation of students who were imparted education by an Acharya. The first test to which a pupil was subjected to was the admission test. It has been repeatedly reiterated at several sutras that no pecuniary benefit shall accrue to the teacher by way of imparting education as it will mean selling of the sacred knowledge for wordly gain and has been condemned by several preceptors. Since there was no consideration or any monetary gain by way of realizing the fee, the admission of the pupil by an Acharaya was based upon the merit and fitness of the student. The basis of judging the same has been reflected as following:

1. In a passage Manu advises that even in the absence of the means of livelihood, a vedic preceptor should rather die with his knowledge than sowing in barren soil.

2. The goddess[17] of learning approached to a Brahman and said to him- "I am thy highest treasure, don't impart me to the person of malign but to him, whom thy shall know to be pure free from the follies of the world and attentive."

Vashista also advises that learning should not be imparted to a wicked member or to one of known uncontrolled passion.

This shows that the following consideration would govern the admission of a student to the studentship of an Acharaya whose judgment with regard to aptitude of student was complete and absolute:

1. Moral fitness : The pupil would be sensible and of controlled passion. He should be simple and pure in heart and amenable to strict discipline of Brahmacharya.

2. Mental Aptitude: He should not be dull, incapable of learning knowledge but should have alert mind and adequately intelligent.

The judgment of Acharya with regard to fulfilling the above merits was complete and total and this was how the admission was given to a student aspirant of admission.

CONTINUOUS ASSESSMENT

The entire course of Vedic study was not of continuous type stretching to a long term of twelve years but was a graduated one divided into several parts which may be termed as modules in modem terminology. Each of such modules was to commence with a Vrata. The duration of these Vrata extended to even full year or so. The teacher would carefully watch the progress of students and his inner capacity by Vratas and also his academic performance. The main Vratas to be observed by students have been mentioned as under:

1. *Savitra Vrara:* This refers to the introduction of Savitri Verse to the student.
2. *Sukriya Vrata* : This refers to the commencement of the study of the main versa to the student.
3. *Anuvachana* : Which means the way in which Vedas are to be studied.
4. *Sakvara: Vritika, etc.*: They refer to the study of Aranyaka and Upanishada Brahamna, *etc.*

The above Vratas suggest that unless the teacher is convinced about the satisfactory completion of study of one module, the commencement of the next module would not ensue. The assessment of the teacher in this regard was final and total.

GRADES OF STUDENTS

The examining Bodies now-a-days are awarding grades to the students on. the basis of one or two terminal examinations. The sutra works provide evidence that the students completing the course of study, who were called 'Snatakas' were also placed into three grades. The normal period of studentship was prescribed as twelve years on completion of which a student was supposed to bathe as per the ceremony of 'Samavartana' and was called Snataka. Thereafter, he would enter 'Grihistha Ashrama'—the second stage of life and ceases to a Brahmachari. There are three categories of Snatkas mentioned under Gobhila:

1. Vidya Snataka
2. Vrata Snataka
3. Vidya Vrata Snataka

VIDYA SNATAKAS

Those who complete their study of Veda and bathe before the normal period of studentship.

VRATA SNATAKAS

Those were just the reverse kind who bathe before completing their study but they have completed the normal period of studentship.

VIDYA VRATA SNATAKAS

Those who complete the prescribed period of Brahmacharya and also their study.

This suggests the three grades of students:

1. Intellectually brilliant students complete their whole study before the lapse of the period of studentship i.e. twelve years and are called Vidya Snatakas.
2. Medium students from intellectual point of view finish their study just in twelve years and are called Vidya Vrata Snatakas.
3. Below average students who fail to complete their study obviously give up a part prescribed period of twelve

years. Such students obviously give up a part of their study though they are also Snatakas but are called Vrata Snatakas.

This is exactly similar to modem grade system under which a 'Board of Examinations' does not declare a student pass or failed but he is given a grade. It is interesting to infer from the above that under the ancient system whatever finished was finished thoroughly to the satisfaction of teacher and the student was having complete knowledge of that which has been covered by him.[18] However, under the modem system a student acquires a certain percentage of knowledge of the whole course but not the complete knowledge of any subject.

PANINI'S METHOD OF EXAMINATION

Panini-a great grammarian of the ancient period is the pioneer of the period of Sutra education. In fact this period is supposed to start with Panini's grammatical literature which gives some evidence on the education system as well as examination system. Ashtadhyayi' is one of the famous works of Panini in which the conditions of the period are reflected that grew with the grammar of Panini. The work of Panini has attracted two famous preceptors Katyayana and Patanjali who compiled two famous commentaries 'Vartika' and 'Mahabhasaya' respectively which are important in the field of education.

CLASSIFICATION OF STUDENTS:

From the above three books i.e. Ashtadhyayi, Vartika, Mahabhasaya, it teanspires that the students were classified as under from intelligence point of view:

1. Srotriya
2. Vednam student

Srotriya[18(a)] were the persons or students who learnt the various scriptures by rot method including the Chhanda of Vedas. Such students who simply committed to memory without understanding the meaning were also called patham pathi.

Vednam. The term applied to the knowledge of the meaning of the word or text of Veda.

This shows that the study of Vedas was carried out by rot learning method. However there were some subjects of study where learning played a secondary role and understanding of the subject was important.

Unique Method of Examination: Panini appears to be the pioneer in introducing a technique of examination. In fact he is the first one to have introduced the system of terminal examination at the end of study. There are two sutras of Panini to denote the system of examination. The performance of a student was judged from his capacity to remember and repeat the text without any fault and the students were placed in

Question paper (oral)

A. Question paper comprises of Vedic text selected at the diseretion of the teacher

B. The answer script was the recitation of text by the student.

C. Evaluation was based upon the accuracy of recitation of text

D. The result of student was placed in grades.

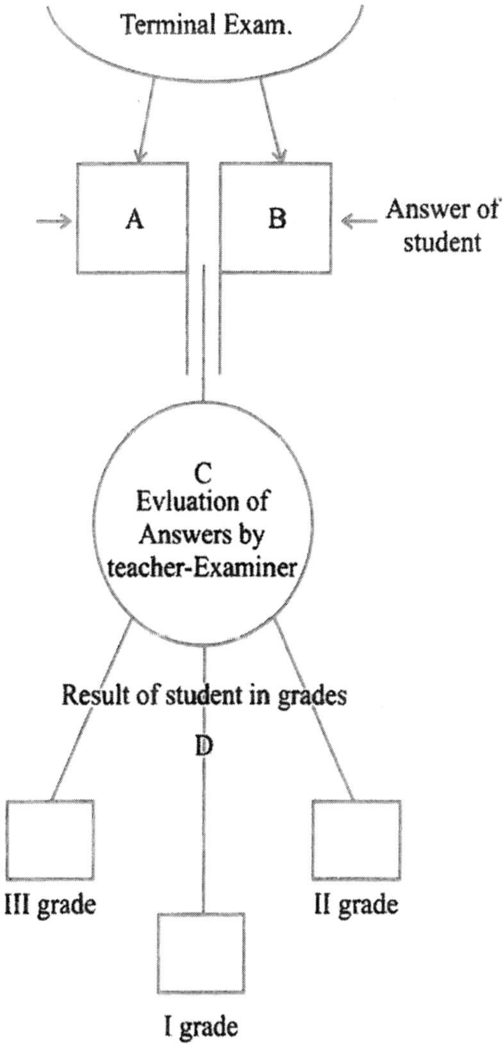

Evaluation System of Panini

different grades depending upon the mistakes committed by them in reciting the text of Veda or a Chhanda. A student who committed one mistake at the time of examination was called Aikanyika i.e. one error student[19]. Similarly that who committed *two* errors was given the grade of Divanyika', the two error student and so on. These grades were based upon the number of errors thus made by a student which could go upto 12 and student was called dwadasanyika student[20]. There is no mention of further apithets which show that there.were 12 grades for ranking the students and those committing more than 12 errors were assumed as failed. It is also obvious from the above that the text which was given to the students—the examinees for recitation, were chosen at the discretion of the teacher. The examination technique appears to be perfect and assessment of the performance was also fool proof. It satisfies all the requirements of the modem method of evaluation under which the question paper is set from a chapter of a text book at the discretion of the teacher and the student's ability is judged from the answer given by him on the script book which are evaluated by the teacher and marks are assigned.

Negative marking: The method of evaluation introduced by Panini may be called as a negative marking for very solid reasons. In those days almost a hundred percent accuracy was expected from the students in respect of recitation of texts. in fact during the Vedic and later Vedic period a single error committed by the priest in respect of recitation of the Vedic hymn was taken so seriously that he was disqualified from performing any further ritualistics of Vedas.

KAUTILYA'S METHOD OF ASSESSMENT AND CLASSIFICATION OF STUDENTS

Kautilya is one of the important alumni of Sutra period during 4th Century B.C. His famous work 'Arthasastra' throws some light over his views on education and assessment of students. Kautilya is regarded as the minister of Chandragupta Maurya who got the latter enthroned destroying the dynasty of Nandas, It can be safely concluded that Kautilya was the author of the 'Arthasastra' which gives some information on paedegogy.

His views on learning are very original according to which learning can be imparted through discipline upon a suitable stuff. On assessment and classification of students, he mentions three kinds of students as under:

1. The students were been adjudged to have sharp intelligence, if they are able to carry into practice whatever is taught to them concerning righteousness and wealth.

2. Stagnant intelligent students - those who are unable to put into practice the good instructions taught to them.

3. Perverted minded students - those who instead of putting into practice the good instructions entangle themselves into dangerous and other perverted aspects of the instructions imparted to them, are termed as perverted minded students.[2]'

In view of the fact, that Kautilya was the Minister of Chandragupta and wielded a lot of influence in his period, the classification of students and therefore, the method of assessment of students must have been implemented in the schools under the empire of Chandragupta. The number of schools which have been named after their founders many of them should have been following the classification of students as mentioned by Kautilya.

REFERENCES

1. **Manusmriti IV-110.**
   i.b.i.d. - 113 and 126
2. **Chhand, Upanishadas V.II.5**
3. मनु: 2/140
   तद् यस्मात् स आचार्यः ॥११॥ वेदानुवचनाच्च॥
   गौ.ध.सू. १।११-१२
4. एकादेशं तु वेदश्य वेदाङ्गापि वा पुनः।
   योऽध्यापयति वृत्त्यर्थमुपाध्यायः स उच्यते। मनुः 2।1।41
5. 2. त्रंविद्या हेतुकस्तर्को नैरूक्तो धर्मपाठकः।
   त्रयश्चा श्रमिणाः पूर्वे परिषत्स्याद् दशावरा ॥१११॥
   Manu XII-iii
6. **Sacred Books of Eatst, Vol. XXV.**
   (by Bubler)
7. वर्जयेन्मधु मांसं च गन्धं माज्ल्यं रसान् स्त्रियः
   शुक्नित यानि सर्वाणि प्राणिनां चैव हिजंसनम्॥ म. स्मृ. ॥-177
   अभ्यङ्गमञ्जनं चाक्ष्णोरूपानच्छत्रधारणम् म. स्मृ ॥-178
   कामं क्रोधं च लोभं च नर्तनं गीतवादनम्।
   द्यूतं च जनबादं च परिवादं तथानृतम् ॥ म.स्मृ. ॥-178-171

7(a) वेदास्त्यागश्च यमाश्च नियमाश्च तपांसि च।
न विप्रदुष्टभावस्य सिद्धिं गच्छतिकहिचित्॥ मनु. 2197

7(b) कालः क्रीडनकं ते तदन्तेऽध्ययनस्य च।
विष्णु पुराण ।-12-18

8. उपनयनं विद्यार्थस्य श्रुतितः संस्कार॥9॥
   वसन्ते ब्राह्मणमुपनयीत, ग्रीष्मे राजन्यं,

शरदि वैश्यं, गर्भाष्टमेषु ब्राह्मणं
गर्भैकादशेषु राजन्यं गर्भद्वादशेषु वैश्यम्॥19॥

आपस्तम्ब ध.सू. 1।1।1।9, 19

9. तस्मिन्नभिजन विद्यासमुदेतं समाहित संस्करतारमीप्सेत्।
तस्मिंश्चैव विद्या कर्मान्त मविप्रतिपन्ने धमभ्य:।
यस्माद् धर्मानाचिनोति स आचार्य:॥ तस्मै न द्रु ह्येत्कदाचन्॥
स हि विद्यातस्तं जनयति॥ तच्छ्रेष्ठं जन्म॥
शरीरमेव मातापितरौ जनयत:॥ शास्त्रैरधिगतानामिन्द्रिय दौर्बल्याद्
विप्रतिपन्नानां शास्ता निर्वेषमुपदिशेद् तथाकर्म यथोक्तम्॥
आपस्तम्ब ध.सू. 11112-17; 2।5।10।12
तद् द्वितीयं जन्म ॥10॥ गौतम 1।10

॥7॥

नं चेदभ्युदियात्सूर्य: शयानं कामचारत:।
निम्लोचेद्वाप्यविज्ञानाज्जपन्नु पवसेद्दिनम्॥ म.समृ. ॥-220

10. **Manu II-113**

   A. **Manu II-10, XI-264**
   B. **Manu III-185**
   C. **Manu XI-33**
   D. **Manu II-140**
   E. **Manu III-232**

11. सूर्येण ह्यभिनिर्मुक्त: शयानोऽभ्युदितश्चचय:।
प्रायश्चित्तमकुर्वाणो युक्त: स्यान्महतैनसा। म.स्मृ. ॥-221

12. उपेतस्याचार्यकुले ब्रह्मचारि वास: ॥11॥
अष्टाचत्वारिशद् वर्षाणि ॥12॥
पादूनम् ॥13॥
अर्धेनं त्रिभिर्वा ॥14॥
द्वादशावरार्ध्यम् ॥15॥
न ब्रह्मचारिणो विद्यार्थस्य परापवासोऽस्ति ॥17॥

13. श्रावण्यां पौर्णमास्यामध्यायमुपाकृत्य मासं प्रदोषे नाधीयीत ॥1॥
तैष्यां पौर्णमास्यां रोहिणयां वा विरमेत् ॥2॥
अर्ध पञ्चमां श्चतुरो मासानित्येके ॥3॥
आपस्तम्ब ध.सू. 1।1।2।11-17; 1।3।9।1-3
द्वादश वर्षाण्येक वेदे ब्रह्मचर्य चरेत् ॥52॥
प्रतिद्वादश वा ॥53॥
सर्वेषु ग्रहणान्तं वा ॥54॥
श्रवणादि वार्षिकं प्रोष्टपदीं वोपाकृत्याधीयीतच्छन्दांसि ॥1॥
अर्धपंचमान् मासान् पंच दक्षिणायनं वा ॥2॥
गौतम ध.सू. 2।52-54; 16।1-2

14. **Manu-II-73**
Ashta. V.2.84

15. गुरूणानुमतः स्नात्वा समावृत्तो यथाविधि।
उद्वहेत द्विजो भार्यां सवर्णां लक्षणान्विताम्॥ म.स्मृ ॥।-

16. स्नास्यंस्तु गुरूणाज्ञप्तः शक्त्या गुर्वर्थमाहरेत्
क्षेत्रं हिरण्यं गामश्वं छत्रोपानहमासनम्।
धान्यं शाकं च वासांसि गुरवे प्रीतिमावहेत्॥
म.स्मृ. ॥-245-246

17. विद्या ब्राह्मणमेत्याह शेवधिष्टेऽस्मि रक्षमाम।
असूयकाय मां मादास्तथा स्यां वीर्यवन्तमा॥ मनुस्मृतिः ॥-114
यमेव तु शुचिं विद्यात्रियत्रब्रह्मचारिणम्।
तस्मै मां बूहि विप्राय निधिपायाप्रमादिने॥ म.स्मृ. ॥-115

18. अप्रतिभायां यावन्तं कालं न वेद तावन्तं कालं तदधीयीत।
यदा जानापादुंषतो यजुष्टः सामत इति ॥6।
बौधायन ध.सू. 1।9।6

18 (a) Ashta V.2.84.

19. कर्माध्ययने वृत्तम्। अष्टा. iv-4-63
ऐकन्यिकः यस्याध्ययने प्रवृत्तस्य परीक्षाकाले विपरीतोच्चारणरूपं स्खलितमेकं जातं सः। सि.कौ. 327
अष्टा. iv-4-64

20. द्वादशान्यानि कर्माण्ध्ययने वृत्तान्यस्य
द्वादशान्यिकः द्वादशापपाठाः अस्य जाता इत्यर्थः।
सि.कौ. - 327

21. शिष्यमाणो धर्मार्थावुपुलभते चानुतिष्टति च बुद्धिमान्। उपलभमानो नानुतिष्टत्याहार्यबुद्धिः। अपायनित्यो धर्मार्थद्वषी चेति दुर्बुद्धिः। अ.शा. I-17.

7

Ancient Centres of Learning and Universities

7

ANCIENT CENTRES OF LEARNING AND UNIVERSITIES

Fig.1

In Ancient India there were grand seats of learning well comparable to modem universities where eminent and accomplished men assembled in number and attained excellence in their disciplines of study and became famed for their wisdom. These universities attracted students from foreign countries, who on completing their studies were beholden with great respect being the scholar of that university[1], similar to a Harward or a Full bright scholar in modem times who has studied in these universities of U.S.A.

The universities of Ancient India were not the hutments of mud and bushes but some of them were comprised of grand buildings even multi- storeyed ones, magnificent libraries and congenial natural surroundings inside and outside. Some of the universities were characterised by wonderful entrance gates guarded by dwarpanditas[2] who were also learned personalities capable to screen the incoming students in regard to their fitness for study.

METHODS OF EXAMINATION AND TESTS

The ancient Indian universities were marked by unique methods of tests and examinations followed by them for evaluating the educational attainment of students. Some of the methods of test and examination of the ancient Indian universities were as under:

1. Dwarpandita method of test
2. Shalkha Priksha method
3. Dialectical skill method

These methods have been explained in detail in the following pages of the chapter. What is more remarkable is the fact that some of the universities of ancient India were awarding diploma to the passing out students contrary to the usual belief that no examinations were conducted in ancient India and no diploma or degree were conferred upon passing students.

Following are the famous universities and seats of learning in ancient India:

TAXILA

AN OLDEST CENTRE OF LEARNING - A UNIVERSITY

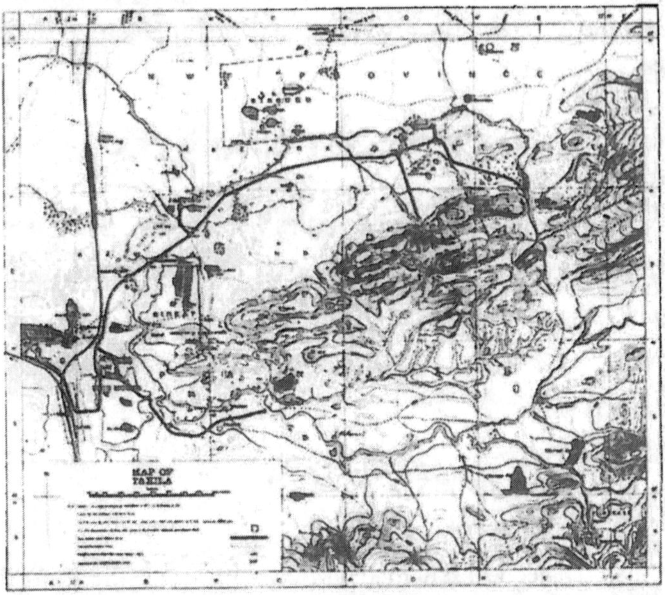

Remains of TAXILA

This is considered to be the oldest of all the ancient seats of learning — a Brahmanic intellectual centre since the time of *Ramayana*[3] and *Mahabharata*[4] where it has been referred to as a famous seat of learning. Takshila or Taxila was situated in North West India now in Pakistan near Rawalpindi and was the capital of Gandharga. This has been the native land of Panini the great grammarian of ancient times, India has ever produced. Taxila or Takshila is named after Taksa—the ruler son of great king Bharta. As per reference of *Mahabharata,* Janamejaya's 'Serpent sacrifice Gayna' was performed ज this very place. At the time of invasion of Alexander it was the noted seat of learning and the Greeks who then came in contact with Brahman philosphers were amazed at their excellence of doctrines. At the time of Buddha when the Muhammadan invasions burst upon India such excellent centres of learning were destroyed scattering the students here and there.

SET UP OF THE UNIVERSITY

Taxila University comprised of numerous schools each run by a renowned teacher. In fact Taxila shot into world wide fame on account of the teachers who were the acknowledged authority in their subjects. There were schools for specialized disciplines i.e. School of Medicine and School of Archery, etc. which were rated as the best for training in these fields.

SUBJECTS OF STUDY

The colleges at Takshila were not meant for beginners or secondary school level. The University was the seat for higher education. As transpires from Jatakas, normally the students at the age of sixteen were sent there and it was a big sacrifice for the parents to send their sons thousands of miles away from home, for advanced studies. As per Jatakas* and Milinda Panha, the 3 Vedas and 18 Arts and professions (Sippas) were taught at Takshila. However, the details of the courses are not given. From the perusal of different Jatakas[5] we infer the following disciplines as were being offered for studies:

Technical Education[5(a)]	(i)	Military Science
	(ii)	Medicine
Crafts/Vocation[5(b)]	(i)	Elephant Lore
	(ii)	Hunting
Liberal Arts[5(c)]	(i)	Magic Charms
	(ii)	Divining from signs of the body
	(iii)	Spell for bringing back the dead to life
	(iv)	Logic
	(v)	Astrology
	(vi)	Astronomy
	(vii)	Accountancy
	(viii)	Commerce
	(ix)	Charm for commanding all things of senses, etc.

The duration of courses was varying upto 7-8 years as in the case of Jivaka who studied medicine for seven years.

ADMISSION OPEN TO ALL

NO TEST

From the stories as mentioned in various Jatakas, the admission was open to all with no test for entrance. It appears that one of the considerations for the open door policy had been that the aspirant students had to travel a distance of hundreds and even thousands of miles to reach Taxila. With no means of transport available in those days it would take months to complete the journey which was some time perilous also. It is only the intensive desire and sincerity to persure advanced study and the willingness to make sacrifice in terms of comfort, luxury, etc. which brought the students at the portal of the college at Taxila. Such being the case the denial of admission would have been grossly unfair to a true seeker of knowledge.[6]

TUITION FEE

As regards the payment of tuition fee the usual rate appears to be one thousand pieces of money for the entire duration of the course[6(a)] and this would cover boarding and lodging also. The fee was payable in advance. In fact the practice had the validity as the teacher was to provide meals and shelter to the student also and the amount of fee was to cover by and large the cost of meals only. In fact no student was denied admission because of his inability to pay fee in cash. Such a student was allowed to pay in shape of menial service to his teacher. The number of students who would attend to the service of their teacher in the day and attending classes in night was quite large. Sometimes philanthropic institutions or individuals would come forward to bear the expenses of education of poor students[6(b)].

SYSTEM OF TEACHING

The theoretical instructions were imparted through lectures and discussions. However, the theoretical course was followed by practical exercises. There appear to be rigorous practical, done by the students for mastering the skill especially in the case of medical science, etc. The instance of Jivaka, a student of medical science who after completing his course of seven years performed difficult operations of surgery while returning home, which would have otherwise not been possible had he not perfected the art of surgery during the course of his training at Takshila, proves it. In case of liberal arts there appears to be a practice that after completing the theoretical and practical course the student would go round the country to put his skill into practice. In Jatakas there are several instances when the students having been trained in different sciences at Takshila would leave that place with the intention of practical applications at country site. Jataka 115 mentions of a prince of Kosala who after studying the different arts at Takshila left the place to study practical uses of the skill, he mastered. Similarly another[7] Jataka confirms the practice containing another such instance where a Brahman student having been specialized in archery went to Andhra Country to put his art of archery into practice.

TEST AND EVALUATION

Takshila was not like a modem university nor did it had the colleges accredited to it in modem sense nor the curricula were being followed in different schools or colleges at Takshila having been prescribed by the university. It was a renowned centre of learning. Each of the teacher who had authoritative knowledge of a subject and assisted by his advanced students formed an institution by itself. There was no system of terminal examination. Students were having the liberty to terminate their study at their option.

UNIQUE METHOD OF EXAMINATION

For specialized courses like Medicine and Surgery or Military Art which were very important for human life and human protection, there must have been methods to test the competence of the students to practise that art or technology at the completion of the courses. One such instance has been traced which speaks the unique method being followed to test that the student did have the skill and knowledge of the subject.

Jivaka was a student of medical science at Takshila who on completion of seven years of his studies had to undergo such test, when his teacher asked him "Take this spade" said he "and seek round about Takshila in yojana on every side and whatever plants you see which arc not medicinal bring it to me." Jivaka as a sincere and competent studcnt walked round the city with spade in hand but every plant he examined was found to have some or the other medicinal use. He accordingly returned to his teacher to report the fact to him. The teacher was satisfied that his pupil did possess the requisite knowledge and he was permitted to go home to practise the medical science.

By this method it appears the teacher had satisfied himself that his pupil had imbibed the real knowledge of the medical science and he knows the use of every plant from the medicinal point of view which was a very important component of medical science in ancient India.

In case of military science or archery there are references in several Jatakas that in one of the schools[7(a)] of archery there were one hundred and three princes under going training hailing from different parts of the country. There must have been some device to test the skill of a trainee in the art before he was allowed to go.

FALL OF TAKSHILA

Takshila appears to be flourishing with educational activities till 250 A.D. and declination came in thereafter. At the end of 5th century A.D. Hanavalanche ruined it completely.

NALANDA UNIVERSITY

(450 A.D. to 850 A.D.)[8]

Fig.3

Nalanda University which came to flourish as a Centre of learning towards the middle of 5th Century A.D. is 40 miles to the South West of Patna. The credit to develop Nalanda as the greatest University and Buddhist Monastery goes to Gupta Rulers.

The University comprised of a Central College with 7 halls attached to it. The building of Viharas was as high as touching the cloud.

There was a compound wall around the whole colony with a door on southern side. As per "Life" (Page iii) the gates opened into the great college. The buildings were having richly adorned towers looking like hill top with their height touching the sky. There was transluent ponds blossomed with blue lotus and at intervals the arnra grove spread over their shade. As per observation of I-T. Siang there were eight halls and three hundred apartments[9].

Nalanda had a grand library which was situated in a special area called 'Dharma Ganja' and was nine-storeyed high. The library was having a rich collection of rare and sacred books on different subjects.

Nalanda owned hundreds of villages yielding rich revenue. As per Hiuen-T. Siang. lodging, boarding, clothing and medicines were free to the students on account of rich endowments made by the contemporary rulers. The University was ruined by muslim invaders towards the end of 12th century A.D. The buildings were destroyed and a large number of people were massacred.

There were supposed to be 5000 monks studying in the middle of 7th century A.D.

The head priest of Nalanda was a highly celebrated and reputed man—Dharamapala and Chandrapala. Gunamatic and Sthriamatic are the notable figures among contemporaries.

CURRICULUM OF NALANDA UNIVERSITY

Nalanda was the centre of higher learning in advance studies, so much so that Hiuen-T. Siang a scholar and a Chinese traveller who was already 'master of law' travelled to undertake a perilous journey to India to stay here for study. The curriculum was not confined to the study of the Buddhist religion, philosophy and literature but covered almost the entire circle of knowledge that was available. It included the work belonging to eighteen seets, the Vedas, the Hetu Vidya, Shabada Vidya i.e. Sanskrit, Grammar, the Chikitsa Vidya (medicine), Atharva Veda and Magic, etc. Also the study pursued by Hiuen T. Siang indicates that philosophical logic and astrological subjects as well as yoga shastra were also covered in the curriculum followed at Nalanda. Hiuen T. Siang himself was the student of the yoga shastra in which Shail-bhadra the Chancellor of the Nalanda University was considered to be an authority.

THE SYSTEM OF EDUCATION

The education imparted at Nalanda was free. The boarding, lodging, clothing and medicine were also free. The expenditure on this account was free and was met from the income of estate consisting of hundreds of villages endowed by the then ruler.

In fact the students had not to worry about their material needs of life and this enabled them to concentrate on their studies whole heartedly.

TEACHING SYSTEM

In this regard Hiuen-T. Siang[10] remarks as under:

"That the pupil after attending to the service of his teacher reads a part of scripture and reflects on what he has learnt; he acquires new knowledge day by day and searches into odd subjects month after month without losing a minute. He further says that after studying grammar, etc. under instructors they pass two or three years at Nalanda or in the Country of Valabhi (Western India). It appears grammar was taken as the foundation of all other studies and an elementary knowledge of the same was considered necessary before entering Nalanda."

Regarding the quality of education and the calibre of the students passing various courses of study, Hiuen-T. Siang describes as under:

"The priests, to the number of several thousands are men of the highest ability and talent. Their distinction is very great at the present time, and there are many hundreds whose fame has rapidly spread through distant regions. Their conduct is pure and unblameable. They follow in sincerity the precepts of the moral law. The rules of their

conduct are severe and all the priests are bound to observe them. The countries of India respect them and follow them. Day was not sufficient tor asking and answering questions from morning till night. They engage in discussions, the old and the young, mutually helped each other."

ADMISSION

As transpired from the contemporary literature or history, Nalanda University had the department of Secondary Education also, though it was the prime centre of advance learning and higher studies. The admission of students for Secondary Education was made free without any test. However, students admitted for advanced courses at the age of twenty" or so were admitted only on their passing the test which was oral in nature. The students not only from India but from Mangolia and even from other distant countries like China, Koria, Tibet, etc. used to come to the University to put an end to their doubts and thereby becoming celebrated scholars.

TESTS AND EVALUATION OF STUDENTS

Nalanda being a centre of advance studies with unique reputation, there was a big rush of students seeking admission to the various courses being offered by the University for study. As such, admission to the University was regulated through conducting an entrance test of high standard keeping with the name of the University. The portals of the schools of discussions were guarded by the learned persons well-versed in the discipline concerned and the aspirant students for admission had to undergo oral test and were put some hard questions in judge their knowledge and fitness *for* the course of study. The standard was so high that majority of the students would fail to answer the difficult questions and only twenty percent or so could succeed in obtaining admission on passing the test. An excerpt from Hiuen T. Siang reads as under:[11]

"Of those from abroad who wished to enter the schools of discussion the majority beaten by the difficulties of the problems withdrew, and those who were deeply versed in old and mode learning were admitted, only two or three out of ten succeeding."

As regards evaluation of students undergoing various courses of study, a student would memorize the course to commit to memory everything, he was taught. However, the higher part of the course comprising of discussion and debate, the evaluation of the student as done on the basis of his ability to vanquish the opponents in discussion. In fact, the students after leaving the University became renowned and far famed on the basis of their excellence in this art. I.T. Siang says: "And there the eminent and accomplished men assemble in crowds, discuss possible and impossible doctrines, and after having been assured of the excellence of their opinions by wise men, become far famed for their wisdom to try the sharpness of their wit they proceed to the King's Court to lay down before it the sharp weapon of their abilities, then they present their schemes and show their (Political) talent, seeking to be appointed in the practical Government. When they are present in the House of Debtate, they raise from their seat and seek to prove their wonderful cleverness. When they are refuting heretical doctrines all their opponents become tongue tied and acknowledge themselves undone. Then the sound of their renown flows as it were over the four borders. They receive grants of land and are advanced to a high rank, their famous names are, as a reward written in white on the lofty gates."

AWARD OF DEGREE

In fact, no degree or diploma was awarded to the outgoing student. However, the students of Nalanda were looked upon as model all over India. As such the fellowship of Nalanda was considcred as an academic degree. For this reason the name of Nalanda which was a degree itself, was stolen to receive honour and respect.

WAS ANY TERMINAL EXAMINATION HELD AT NALANDA?

Nalanda University was catering for higher learning and training in the arts of disputation and public speaking, for aiding in solution of doubts. It was almost a research institute. The fellowship of which was coasidered as a passport of fame. The foreign students came from many distant countries like China, Korea, Tibet and Mangolia, etc. for securing valuable Mss and putting to an end to their doubts and to earn fame as scholars.

In view of the above, holding any terminal examination was meaningless and not being relevant to the nature of studies under taken by the students.

UNIVERSITY OF VIKRAMASHILA (850 A.D. to 1203 A.D.)

The University owes its start to King Dharampala who got the Vihara constructed with hundred eight temples

Fig. 4

somewhere at the close of the eighth century A.D. The site selected for the purpose was a wonderful one located on a hillock on the bank of the river Ganges in North Magdha in Bihar. Thc university was maintained with the rich grants *endowed* by the King.

SET-UP OF THE UNIVERSITY

The Campus of the University[12] was encircled by a strong wail around it with hundred eight temples and six colleges and a Central Hall which was called as the house of Sum and was having six gates each opening to a college. The wails of the University were painted with portraits of distinguished scholars who were par excellence for their learning and character. They were rewarded in this manner and were conferred upon thc title of 'Pandit' by the King himself.

FUNCTIONING OF THE UNIVERSITY

A striking feature of the functioning of the University was that a board of eminent teachers was formed to control the teaching. The total number of teachers including those controlling the day to day affairs of teachers were hundred and eighteen in number who were appointed by the King. It is also said that there were eminent teachers who were working both for the Nalanda University and Vikramashila University. The president of the University was always a learned and a pious personality.

ADMISSION AND ACADEMICS

There was a unique system to control the admission to the six colleges of the University. It transpires that the gate of the each college was guarded by 'Dwarpanditas' who were the Scholars of eminence. The names of the gate keepers in the time of 'Chanka' as given by historians were as under:

1. Ratnakarasanti, East Gate
2. Vagisvarakirti of Benaras, West Gate
3. Naropa, North Gate
4. Pratankararnati, South Gate
5. Ratnavajira of Kasmira, First Central Gate
6. Jnanasrimitra of Ganga, Second Gate

TEST AND EVALUATION

There was good coordination between the management of Nalanda University and Vikramashila. As the supreme administrative authority i.e. the King was the common head for both, the system of admission followed for Nalanda University must have been the same for Vikaramashila also. There were Dwar Panditas seated at the portal of each college to monitor the admission and the methodology being that a student aspirant for admission into any of the col leges was put oral questions to judge his aptitude and basic knowledge and it was only on passing the test which means, answering the questions satisfactorily he was allowed admission. In India where the paedegogic principle of oral teaching has been traditional, the methodology of test would also be obviously oral.

MITHILA UNIVERSITY

This is the first ancient Indian University to have introduced the system of 'Graduate Examination' for declaring a student as having completed his study.

Mithila is known from the time of Upanishada as a stronghold of Brabmanical culture. King Janaka famous for his philosophical knowledge, was the ruler of Mithila also called Vidcha—the birth place of Sita who was also named as Vaidehai in the age of *Ratnayana.* During the period of *Mahabharta* also Mithila was well known for its brahamanical culture.

Mithila as a seat of learning traces the history when a School of New Logic was founded in eleventh century A.D. by Gangesa Upadhaya. It was further promoted by Mahashwara Tkikum in the times of Akbar.

Mithila as a seat of learning chequed an all India reputation attracting students from far and wide for advanced studies in logic or Nyaya.

SYSTEM OF EXAMINATION

Mithila University introduced a unique system for evaluating the competence of students to mark the completion of his study. This is called "Salaka Priksha" method (Needle examination method). Under this system the candidate was put to test by asking him to explain a page of manuscript and the page was chosen by piercing a needle revolving through the manuscript and the text pierced last by the needle was given to the candidate to explain the same. This method of examination is, in fact, the foundation of modem system of examination under which the student is given to explain the questions set secretly totally unknown to the student and from the given curriculum and a student is asked to explain the same in the examination hall. Under the ancient system of examination being followed by Mithila University, the essential elements of the system were the same. The student who would explain the given page chosen through piercing the needle satisfactorily was awarded the diploma of Mithila University. In fact for ranking of student the same method was followed and a great scholar Vasudeva Sarvabhauma who went to Mithila for specializing in logic was asked to explain all the hundred pages pierced by the needle which he did excellently well and was awarded "Sarvabhama" (knowing all) in recognition of his excellent performance.

One of the peculiar practice followed by the University was that teachers would not allow to take out any copy of the text taught to the students. This was being done to preserve the monopoly of thc University for its specialized courses of study in logic.

NADIA UNIVERSITY
(Dialectical method or Evaluation)

Nadia was located on a site close to the modern town of Krishan Nagar in West Bengal and is renowned from the earliest days for its centre of learning of Brahmanic Education[13].

School of logicians was, founded by Roughupatha Shiromony an eminent scholar and this school has been the 'Alma Mater' of many scholars adding lustre to Nadia University. Then there was department of Astronomy inaugurated by Raghunandana and Ramarudra Vidhanidhi respectively also a school of Tantric studics established at Nadia.

METHOD OR TEACHING

The teaching was imparted through discussions and debate. This has been our traditional method of advancement of knowledge. The students usually learnt by heart the text studied by them through putting questions by the students and this was the usual methodology being followed at these schools.

METHOD OF EVALUATION

Dialectical skill was the main consideration for evaluating the students' knowledge. In fact Nadia University was shot in fame when its first student Raghunatha defeated his teacher of Mithila in arguments. The chair of professorship was given to a candidate who silenced his opponents in an open debate. A student was deemed to be successful, if, he could hold his opponents in a discussion in the assembly of students or scholars by adroit arguments. A British professor on seeing the functioning of Nadia University comments[14] "I could not help looking at these unpretending lecture halls with a deep interest, as I thought of the pandits lecturing there, generation after generation of eager inquisitive minds seated on the floor with his 'Corona' of listening pupils round him, the teacher expatiates on those of infinitesimal logic which makes a European's brain dizzy to think of but whose labyrinth with a trained Nadia student will thread with unfaltering precision.

REFERENCES

1. Hiuen T. Siang (Beat's translation) Vol.II 170.
2. Medieaval School of Indian Logic Appendix C by Satish Chandra Vidya Bhushana.
3. RamayanaUttarKhanda 101. 11.
4. Mahabbarta Adipurwa 111. 172.
5. Jataka 356, 219, 415, 87.

* Jatakas several hundreds in number contain more than 500 stories of previous births of Gautani Buddha as it is believed according to Buddhist doctrine that even the great Buddha had to pass through 84000 previous existences before he could become a Buddha. Many of the stories described in Jatakas are quite old and depict common life of ancient India and its economic and social conditions.

5 (a). Jataka 252.

(b). Jataka 47,200.

(c). Jataka 100,510,415.

6. Jataka 252, 378.

(a) Jataka 239.

(b) Jataka 272, 285, 224.

7. Jataka 356.

(a) Jataka 487.

8. Ancient Indian Education, p. 105. by F.E. Keay.

9. (Takakusu's Translation) I.T. Siang p-65.

10. Bibliography - Huen T.Siang pp. 175, 177.

11. (Takaasu ed.) I.T. siang pp. 175, 177.

12. Medieaval School of Indian Logic, Appendix C by Satish Chandra Vidya Bhushana.

13. Nadia Gazetteer, p. 182.

14. Nadia Gazetteer, P. 182.

8

Vocational Education in Ancient India

8

VOCATIONAL EDUCATION IN ANCIENT INDIA

Ancient India was known as 'Golden Bird', by virtue of its prosperity in all spheres, in natural wealth, gold, money and all round progress brought forth richness to the people. Hiuen T. Siang, the famous Chinese Traveller describes in respect of a city, *"There are some hundred houses (families) or so who possess a hundred lakhs,"* and this reputation attracted the foreign invaders, and neighbouring rulers to attack India for looting, plundering and settling over here.

When Sultan Mohammad conquered Bhim Nagar (Kangra) records say —*"Treasures and precious jewels accumulated in it had attained such an amount that the backs of camels would not carry it nor vessels contain it, nor writer's hands record it, nor the imagination of an arithmatician conceive it."*

This phenomenal progress was made by India on account of its trade, indigenous industries, handicrafts, master artisans and craftsmen. Its physicians earned reputation far and wide. Its sculptors and other craftsmen were of top ranking calibre and competence. Its workers evoked rapturous applause from far and wide. V.A. Smith in his book on fine art remarks in respect of the workmanship of Ashoka Pillars[2].

"It would be difficult to find in any country an example of ancient animal sculpture superior or even equal to this beautiful work of art which successfully combines realistic modelling with idea' dignity and is finished."

This all speaks that there was a good system and sound infrastructure of technical training forming the bed rock of indigenous industries of India and truning out the skilled manpower of high standard and quality. But what was the system of Industrial and technical education in ancient India.

Although of the ancient literature does not help much to reveal the entire system. However, from the scattered and casual references, we can gather the idea of various crafts and technologies in vogue in those days and can draw inference regarding the various outfits of imparting technical education in ancient India.

INDUSTRIAL SET UP

Before going into the details of various systems of imparting technical education, it may be mentioned that ancient India was the country of villages with more than 90% of the population residing in rural area.[2(a)] Neither big metropolitan cities nor heavy industries, attuned to mass production were existing. As such separate echelons of technicians consisting of engineers, supervisors, craftsmen as per system being followed now-a-days were out of reckoning and question of separate institutions for imparting training to engineers, sub-engineers and skilled workers does not arise.

In ancient India each village or a group of villages was more or less self sustained. Besides the farmers, there were carpenters, barbers, potters, leather makers who turned out items of general use and also that which were needed for agricultural purposes.

In towns also there were craftsmen practising various arts and crafts of more diversified nature and more specialised and sophisticated one e.g. boat building, wood carving, metal working, etc. In simplest form an industry would consist of a master craftsman assisted by few apprentices and semi-skilled or unskilled workers turning out various items which were sold by them to customers in response to the orders placed by the latter or to the traders directly. There was hardly any distinction between a technician and a craftsman as is existing now a days. It is, however, possible that the role performed by the master craftsmen may be of guiding nature and looking after other management functions. But the system was by and large attuned on domestic[3] lines akin to Indian tradition not the mechanical method of mass pmduction turning out standardized articles.

The craftsmen in town were organized in tradeguilds. The membership of guilds was hereditary and no unqualified person could be a member of a guild which some time controlled the quality or materials and standard of product.

DISCIPLINES OF CRAFTS AND TECHNOLOGY

VEDIC PERIOD

The history of various vocations and crafts as were being pursued in ancient India is as old as Vedic Period. In Rigveda, we have a reference as under:

"We[3(a)] different men have different aptitudes and pursuits. The carpenter deals with broken things, the physician a patient, the priest some one who will perform sacrifice."

No doubt from the period of Rigveda, there is evolution and development of different crafts rather indigenous industries, called so, in modern terminology. These were manned by carpenters, blacksmiths, goldsmiths, tanners, etc. The carpenterwood technician produced the items like carts, chariots, wagons etc. while a blacksmith diversified himself as a metal worker. Another master craftsman would make further advancement and build ships and boats. The mention of a ship in Rigveda having 100 oars confirms it. The metal worker was turning out ploughs, cans, utensils, etc. There is a reference of an iron city and also of a mansion with one thousand[4] pillars which suggests that the craft of masonry later on developed into architecture. In fact Atharva Veda refers to the altars of different architectural shape to be constructed at different occasions.

In nut shell the following disciplines of craft[5] and technology were in vogue for which training was given through different systems as mentioned in later pages:

1. Carpentry
2. Weaving
3. Blacksmithy
4. Goldsmithy
5. Masonry
6. Architecture
7. Boat building
8. Shipbuilding
9. Weaving industry

10. Metal technology
11. Jewellery art
12. Fort building

During Upanishada period the details of the disciplines as were being studied are contained in the reply given by Narada to Sanatkumara which throws ample light on the point.

Narada says that he had studied the subjects[6] like -

1. Rigveda
2. Yajurveda
3. Samveda
4. AtharvaVeda
5. Itihasa Purana
6. Grammar
7. Biology
8. Arithmatic
9. Divination
10. Dialecties
11. Politics
12. Military science
13. Vedangas
14. Astronomy
15. Study of snake vemons
16. Fine arts
17. Ayurveda (Medical Science)

Out of the above list disciplines at S. No. 12 and 15 belong to technical education which were the part of general curriculum. Besides the above the usual crafts and technologies as were existing during Vedic period must no doubt be continuing during Upanishada period also and no significant change was registered.

CATTLE BREEDING—A FAVOURITE CRAFT

During the period of Upanishadas cattle breeding or tending cattles or cows assumed a wide significance and popularity so much so that it formed an important part of Vedic education. One of the essential duty of a pupil on entering into studentship of a preceptor was to tend the cattles/cows of his Guru.

An interesting reference is available in Chhand Upanishada in this regard. Satya-Kama Jabala after he was initiated by his Guru was assigned the job of cow rearing and four hundred weak and lean cows were entrusted to him with the instructions that he would return to his Guru for being imparted education after the four hundred cows grew into one thousand good one and this assignment or the task was carried out most sincerely and competently by Satya-Kama Jabala and he lived in forest for years together rearing and tending the cows till they grew into one thousand healthy ones.

This shows that the craft of cattle breeding was beholden with regard in those days. This craft calls for the expertize and the knowledge of the animal husbandry, veterinary science and dairy farming. The health and breeding of cows and cattles were very important factors. Also the milk from the cows was put into many uses e.g., curd, butter, ghee, ete. and one had to have the propcr knowledge of the processes involved in this regard. It may be mentioned that the preceptor and Acharyas/Guru in those days were maintaining a herd of cows which were looked after by the students receiving education under them. We read of a famous name of Yajna Valyka—a very learncd and knowledgeable Rishi of those days who was rewarded by one thousand cows by the great King Janaka— the Videha, for being the most read and learned person having won the debate on philosophical discussions held by the King. In fact, it was the common practice in those days to gift away hundreds and thousands of cows to the priests,[7] brahmans and Rishis at the occasion of royal functions and tending cows was considered as part of religious duties of every Aryan. It was on account of this phenomenal development of the craft of cattle- breeding that India was regarded a country where milk and curd would flow like rivers.

PERIOD OF SAMRITIS, PANINI AND KAUTILYA

The period is marked with the famous works of Panini—the greatest grammarian of ancient India, Manu, Narada, Gautam Smrities and other preceptors who made their indelible marks on the sands of time. Chanakya or Kautilya who is supposed to be the minister of Chandragupt Maurya and is a renowned figure for his famous work—Arathshastra is also a luminary of this period.

The various crafts and technology registered development, advancement and diversification during the period of Maurya Kings as evinced from Arthshastra of Kautilya'. Though Panini who is considered as the pioneer of this period also gives a brief reference of two types of education i.e. classical education and vocational education called Vritta means that which earns livelihood. As commentcd in 'Panini Kaleen Bharta Varsha, (by Shri V.S. Aggarwal) numerous vocations were in vogue as a result of rising standard of living, however, no precise details have been given except the scattered references.

Kautilya in his Arthshastra mentions[8] the various departments of industries as under which shows the progress of technology in those days:

1. Superintendent of treasury controlling the pearl, jem, diamond indicating the existence of these technologies.
2. Controller of weaving indicating the existence of weaving and textile technology.
3. Superintendent of metals dealing with the manufacture of copper, lead, tin, mercury, brass, etc.
4. Chief of department of mines, controlling the metallurgy industry.

5. Similarly, there was a department of salt, gold and silver, agriculture and Directorate of Navigation indicating that the relevant industries and the technology of ship building were sufficiently developed.

The rising standard of life of people usually calls for advancement and diversification of various crafts and industry. The art and technology of jewellery making and glass making touched all time high level of sophistication as gold, silver, gem and precious stones find prominent mention in the book. Fine fabrics of cotton, wool and silk variety of garments, blankets and skins and beverages of all kinds were manufactured on large scale. Grand palaces, temples, etc. were built by kings and wealthy merchants, which resulted into advancement of construction technology. The other minor industries supplying necessaries of luxurious life such as of pottery, dyeing, confectionery, blacksmithy, weaving, garland making were also continuing.

EPIC PERIOD

During Epic period—the period of *Ramayana* and *Mahabharra* the technical/vocational education and the technological progress was at its zoom so far as ancient India is concerned. The grand palace[8(a)] of King Yudhishtra at Indraprastha was without a parallel. In Ayodhya the capital city of *Ramayana,* the roads leading to the city, the majestic buildings and the royal palaces, are splendid achievements of civil engineering and show technological advancement of the time. A gignatic bridge was build over the ocean between India and Ceylon, the capital of Ravana. The *pushpak* viman a wonderful convoy for Lord Rama to return Ayodha, indicates that aeronautical science was also in advanced stage. A work—Vamanik Prakarnam authored by Rishi Bhardwaj who was perhaps contemporary to Lord Rama has been found to contain the fundamentals of Aeronautic Science. The book confirms that the science was the subject of study and research in those days.

FAVOURITE CRAFTS/TECHNOLOGY

The Epic Period was the age of valour and warfare. As such the disciplines of craft and technology were greatly influenced by the conditions of the age. The crafts relating to war and arms registered significant development. Dhanurveda which included all the skills of fighting i.e. sword welding, shield, archery, club fighting, etc. was the favourite pursuit of Kshatriya kings and rulers. The fabrication technology of these arms i.e. bows, arrows, swords, etc. was also at the high pitch of advancement. The preceptors and Acharyas running ashramas and gurukuls largely imparting Vedic and religious education to the twice born castes were perhaps proficient in arm fabrication. In *Ramayana* and *Mahabharata* there are several references purporting to give divine weapons mainly comprising of bow, arrow, etc. i.e. Dhanusha to the kings and rulers. Lord Rama was given many such divine weapons by Munies and acharyas[9]. In Mahabharata, Arjun underwent penance in forests on completion of which Indra gave him divine weapons.

The other favourite crafts included chariot making and chariot driving which was beholden in great respect and regard. Lord Krishna offered himself to act as charioteer in Mahabharata war, the fiercest battle of ancient India. Similarly, the chariot of Karan was driven by another king—one of the relatives of Pandavas. The technology of fabrication of chariot must also be at a very developed stage as the wars between kings were fought riding on chariot. In Mahabharata, Ariuna fought battle riding on divine chariot. Similarly, all other warriors like Daryodhan, Karan, etc. all were having specially built chariots. In Ramayana during the great war between Lord Rama and Ravana a divine chariot[10] was offered by God Indra to Lord Rama requesting him to ride on and to fight with Ravana as it was felt very difficult to fight and kill Ravana without being on chariot. Karan lost the war on account of poorly maintained condition of the chariot in his possession as one of the wheels of chariot broke away and stranded in mud.

As regards the other disciplines of technology or craft being pursued in those days, an extract from Ramayana sheds ample light. When Bharta—the brother of Lord Rama went in procession to persuade the latter to return to Ayodhya, the following classes of craftsmen— technicians also accompanied him

And all others, and the foremost merchants as well as all the principal classes, joyfully went in quest of Rama and number of gem cutters and goodly potters, weavers and armourers and peacock dancers, savers and perforators of gems, glass makers and workers in ivory, cooks, incense-sellers, well known goldsmiths and wool manufacturers, lathers in tepid water, shampovers, physicians, makers of dhupas, and wine sellers, washermen and tailors and actors.[11]

ERA OF BUDDHISM

Buddhism which was an insignificant sect, registered a big boost and transformed into a world religion under the patronage of mighty emperor Ashoka who struck with the horrors of Kalinga War that saw one lakh people slain, enchristened to Buddhism.

The towering personality of Ashoka and his resolution to Buddhism backed by the vast resources of a mighty empire gave a big impetus to the religion creating a kind of spell of Buddhism and this considerably influenced the crafts and technologies providing a new direction. Construction of monasteries, Vihars, Stupas, and Caves for the residence of monks registered a big boom with the result that construction technology and architecture made phenomenal development and progress. Ashoka himself was a great builder of huge stupas and construction of nearly 84000 stupas is stated to have been done under his instructions.

MONASTERIES AS SCHOOL OF TECHNOLOGY AND CRAFT

During the era of Buddhism big monasteries played a cogent role as schools[12] of craft and technology, as the robes of monks, weaving of cloth for the same, construction of Viharas and other services were carried out by the Bhikhus. As a result loom or weaving technology, and construction technology marked a significant development. When a donor wished to construct Vihara, the Bhikhus were sent on the site of construction as overseer to supervise the construction and to guide the workers regarding the size, forms of various apartments as per rules of the Buddhist order. The appointment was made by a resolution of the order and they were called 'Navahaminsika'. Later on there was a practice that the period of 'Navahamna' i.e. supervision by a Bhikhu was fixed in advance according to the magnitude and volume of work involved in construction of a Vihara which would vary from 2 to 7-8 years and even more.

This all suggests that novice and young Bhikhus were given training on the job in weaving technology, construction of Viharas etc. which were designed to comprise of residence of Bhikhus, offices and other facilities. As the spell of Buddhism became more and more strong, the art and technology of constructing the viharas became more and more advanced and monasteries became almost like a residential colony with thousands of monks residing therein. Thus the technology of civil construction and architecture which found its application therein, also developed.

SIXTY-FOUR KALAS

In many a Buddhist and Jain works there is mention of various arts and vocations which were called as Kalas' and the traditional number has been mentioned as sixty-four, though some works mention more than 64 kalas. The details of traditional 64 kalas have been given in many works such as Kadambri, Kamasutra by Vatsayana, etc. The names of these disciplines many of which belong to technical education have been sorted out from the list of 64 kalas as under:

1. Metallurgy
2. Mine technology
3. Cooking technology
4. Science of archery
6. Leather technology
7. Textile design technology
8. Machine fabrication technology
9. Earth work technology
10. Machine construction technology
11. Ship building technology
12. Textile technology

13. Gold technology
14. Dairy technology
15. Weapon manufacturing technology

SYSTEMS OF TECHNICAL AND INDUSTRIAL EDUCATION

The technical and industrial education was functioning on the following lines in ancient India:

There were five kinds of outfit for instructions in various trades and disciplines of Technical Education

1. Hereditary system
2. Apprentice system
3. Guild system
4. School system
5. Ashrama system

APPRENTICE SYSTEM

In ancient India a master craftsman or a technician practising his trade would admit few students as his apprentices. The student aspiring to be educated or trained in a trade was to approach the master craftsman with a request to admit him as latter's apprentice and the master would usually accept the boy for imparting training or skill in that trade and the apprenticeship would continue till the student has learnt the skill and acquired proficiency. The lodging and boarding was free and the student would reside in the home of his teacher who will treat him as his son and will not withhold any of the secrets of trade from him. The profit of whatever work he may be doing therc would belong to his master[12(a)].

The system assumed a vast popularity in ancient India. So much so that the reputed craftsmen and technicians formed their own school in the trade. There is a mention of a school of sculpture on similar pattern. The profession of architecture developed and some earlier works in architecture are the result of the competent architects produced in such schools. Various handicrafts also made phenomenal advancement in their respective fields. The system appears to be working in Sutra period also, in the time of Manu[13] and Panini.

ADVANTAGES OF SYSTEM

The system has many advantages thereby making it the most important system of ancient India and is still in vogue in various trades. The apprentice resides in his master's home and as such he can observe every point relating to the skill at a very close range and is frec to ask questions from the teacher at any time to remove his doubt at any stage and the technique of the skill can be learnt from the very beginning in the shortest period of time. Contact of few hours a day with the teacher to be trained in a skill as being followed in industrial training institutions, now-a-days, does not stand any comparison. Moreover, in the home of teacher, the personality of the apprentice gets crystallised to learn the trade and he would think, he would work and he would dream in terms of technique of trade.

The rules of Apprenticeship as given by Narada' are as under[14]

1. A young man aspiring to learn the skill of a trade must obtain the permission of his parents first and should settle the period of training in advance. He should then live with his master.

2. The apprentice should be provided free boarding and lodging by the master who should impart him training and should not deploy him on any other work.

3. The master should treat the apprentice as his son.

4. The apprentice should continue with his master till the stipulated time, even if, training is completed earlier.

5. The apprentice should give Pradakshana i.e. gift to his teacher according to his means after he has completed his training. The master will have the first right to employ the apprentice after the completion of training, however, the remuneration will be settled according to the qualification of the.apprentice.

HEREDITARY SYSTEM

Ancient India has been famous for its craftmanship. The skill of a particular craft or trade was handed down from father to son'[5] and it helped to keep up the standard of workmanship. This hereditary system of craft education started from later Vedic period. Subsequently all those engaged in a particular vocation became separated from others as castes and the technical skill developed in each caste was passed on from generation to generation. When the father was a craftsman he would train up his own son from the beginning and the boy would day by day be imbibing the spirit of craftsmanship he was learning.[16] In fact one was morally bound to pursue the craft of his forefathers. For most of the crafts, the knowledge of reading and writing was not required. However, thumb rules pertaining to a skill were learnt by heart. The merit of hereditary system of technical training lies in the fact that the boy was taught by observing and handling real jobs and the father would take a great delight to pass on the skill to his son free from any artificiality.

GUILD SYSTEM OF TECHNICAL EDUCATION

Guild in its simplest form was an organisation of craftsmen or artisans or skilled technicians formed to safeguard the collective interest of that industry or craft or vocation. Guild system has been very old to Indian tradition and perhaps came into being towards the close of later Vedic period. Panini has made a mention of guild by the term Varitta. Gautama in his Smriti refers to the main guild of artisans and other vocations. There is also a mention of an organisation-guild by Kalidas. They were called Sharen[17] and every industry or craft was governed by its Shareni which was having its own laws and rules for safeguarding and administering the interest of the respective industry[18]. The importance of guild lies in the fact that they were not merely a union of craftsmen but had a role in imparting technical education to their members in the highly specialised crafts like ivory, carving, painting, etc. An inference has been drawn that training[19] was also one of the functions of the guild and perhaps a member aspiring of training was attached to a master craftsman running his own industry and also the member of the guild. These guilds became more and more strong and in the age of Buddha both the royal and priestly classes were overshadowed and dominated by these guilds as commented by Dr. B. Prakash in his 'Studies in Indian History & Civilization'.

SCHOOL SYSTEM OF TECHNICAL EDUCATION

Schools imparting education exclusively in technical disciplines developed mostly in the Buddhist and later Buddhist period Takshila University—a name worth reckoning in ancient Indian education was famous for such institutions. There were schools for medical education and school for archery and also exclusive schools for several other discipline which were manned by reputed and renowned teachers— expert in respective subjects. In the school of Archery there is a reference that as many as 103 Princes[20] from all corners of India were imparted education and also the education of a Brahman boy at Takshila University was financed by the King of Benaras. In Jatakas[21] there is a mention that arts and crafts in the undermentioned disciplines were taught in various schools of Takshila University:

1. Medicine 2. Military Science 3. Elephant Lore 4. Hunting 5. Magic Charms 6. Divining from signs of the body 7. Spell for bringing back the dead to life 8. Logic 9. Astrology 10. Astronomy 11. Accountancy 12. Commerce 13. Charm for commanding all things of senses, etc.

Out of the above list only few of the disciplines i.e. archery, etc. belong to the technical education and the remaining are arts or crafts. The teaching of medical sciences at Takshila University/school brought a good name and honour to the latter on account of the famous physician i.e. Jivaka—the personal physician of Lord Buddha who was one of the alumini, of the school.

The method of teaching usually followed at the schools of Takshila University was an improved one. The teaching would begin with the instructions supplemented by practicals. The duration of the course for medical science was of 7 years which means that a comprehensive study was made on all aspects of the science.

Similarly, there are references of Dhanvantri, Narada, Shushrut etc. who were reputed physicians, practising Ayurvedic medicine and have written books and treatises, etc. on various subjects of medical sciences mentioning the symptoms of diseases and their causes and treatment etc. These physicians of ancient India while practising Ayurvedic medicines. formed schools of their own[22] wherein the students were admitted for imparting education in medical sciences. The instructions comprised of not only the practical methods but the theory of the relevant subjects were also explained to them.

ASHRAMA SYSTEM

The Ashramas of Rishies, Preceptors, Acharyas, served as a useful outfit of imparting education in various disciplines including that of Technical Education. The system gained much popularity and currency during the Epic period i.e. during the period of Ramayana and Mahabharaza and this period is called as the age of Ashramas. In fact every preceptor established his own Ashrama which was got extended and expanded with the passage of time and gained the form of an educational institution with royal support and endowments. Some of the ashramas were as large as accommodating tens of thousands of students and were like 'Forest Universities' of Ancient India. As per the evidence of Ramayana and Mahabharata the following Ashramas were mainly functioning during the period:

1. Bhardwaj Ashram at Prayag
2. Balmiki Ashrama
3. Vashisht Ashrama
4. Kanva Ashrama
5. Shounaka Ashrama

These Ashramas were so big and extensive that they were capable to entertain thousands of guests at a time. The Ashrama of Rishi Bhardwaj catered the lodging and boarding of the large entourage of Eharat, brother of Lord Rama consisting of army, residents of Ayodhya, royal guests multi thousands in numbers.[23]

Similarly, the Ashrama of Rishi Balmiki was a very big one and there is mention in Ramayana that Shatrughan the youngest brother of Lord Rama along with his warriors on way to Ayodhya after fighting battle with Lavanashura made his night halt at the Ashrama of Rishi Balmiki.[24] Similarly, Vashishta Ashrama where Lord Rama and his brothers were mostly given education was also very capacious and vast one. Vishvamitra when he was king entered in confrontation with Muni Vashishta and raided and devastated his Ashrama, a large of number students of the Ashrama fled away. It shows that the ashramas were the seats of education of students.

AN ASHRAM

Lav and Kush are being given the training of dhanurveda by Guru Valmiki

EDUCATIONAL SETUP OF A BIG ASHRAMA

As per evidence from Mahabharata a big Ashrama comprised of several departments.

Besides the fire worship and teaching of Vedas, the following departments imparting education in various disciplines were as under:

1. The department of Royal teaching i.e. study of disciplines relevant to a king. Rajniti (Politics) Arithniti (Economics) and Verta (Ethics).
2. Military section.
3. Military Organisation imparting knowledge on forming battalions, Army, etc.
4. Department of Botany.
5. Department of Astronomy.
6. Transport and conveyance.

Military Science education which was an important discipline of Technical Education in those days was catering to the training needs of kings, rulers and their families. The preceptors were well versed in 'Dhanaurveda' which included all branches of Military Science. We read of Balmiki Ashrama where the twin sons of Lord Rama got education by the great Rishi Balmiki. They not only learnt Vedas but were well versed in 'Dhanurvada' also. So much so that they defeated all the great warriors of the army of Lord Rama when the sacrificial horse was captured by them and the army escorting the horse fought fierce battle with Lov and Kush and the renowned warriors like Sugriva even Hanuman, Angadh all were taken captive by them. The Military education which they received, was imparted by Rishi Balmiki in his Ashrama.

This also suggests that the Ashramas of hermits and rishies were the big centres of education including Technical Education and Science of Arms was one of the disciplines of study. From the description of Ashramas some other facts also emerge that the science of catering also developed in the Ashramas some of which were capable to entertain thousands of guests including the royal guests at a time. A reference of *Ramayana* confirms the fact as is seen from the story of King Vishvamitra when he visited the Ashram of Muni Vashista, the latter entertained his large entourage and the Royal guests with various delicacies and dishes which even a modern hotel would envy.

NEW LIGHT ON BHARDWAJ ASHRAM

In recent times discovery of the following old manuscripts of Rishi Bhardwaj on the following subjects sheds a new light on the development of technology and technical education in ancient India.

1. Vaimanik Prakarnam (aeronautical science)
2. Kritka Vajra Nirnay (Preparation of artificial diamonds)

3. Jal Tatva Parakamam (Hydrology)

These manuscripts deal with scientific concepts and seem to be founded on a self contained scientific system of frame work largely unknown to the present system of modern science. In fact they are based on scientific concepts unique to ancient India (See Hindustan Times, dated 25-2-91). The discovery of these manuscripts shows that the technology in ancient India was of highly developed state and the huge Ashram of Rishi Bhardwaj where the education on different disciplines was imparted must be having aeronautics as one of the subjects of teaching.

EXAMINATIONS IN TECHNICAL EDUCATION

The ancient Indian tradition does not consider that a single or double terminal examinations have any value or importance in regard to judging the extent of knowledge of the subject studied by a student, much less in case of technical education or training. Under the domestic system of education or technical training where a student remained under the continuous supervision of the teacher, the latter gets ample opportunity to observe the depth of knowledge of the student. In fact the entire personality of the pupil undergoing training got unobscured to the teacher who would become well aware of the plus points and weak points of the student in respect of a discipline, thereby enabling him to give more emphasis on that aspect including re-explanation of the fundamentals of the topic concerned. The teacher would proceed to the next topic only when the first one is covered and is imbibed adequately by the student.

Under the Indian system the two paedegogic processes were well integrated:

(i) Teaching process
(ii) Evaluation process

The teacher with his constant observation of the student was able to evaluate and to fathom the adequacy of training gained by the student.

As regards examination in technical education, it is all the more necessary that the skill of the trade is thoroughly learnt by a student on all points. Giving a practical exercise to the student on one or two topics and covering certain percentage of the curriculum is hardly a satisfactory device to judge the calibre of student as a technician. In consonance of the above mentioned tradition, there was no meaning of a terminal Examination in a trade or skill or technology. However, there are instances that terminal examinations were conducted in respect of certain disciplines which were of great importance and this is true in case of medical science where we come across of a story of Zivaka.[26]

Zivaka was a student of medical science of Takshila University where the course was supposed to be of seven years' duration, after the end of which the teacher prescribed the following test to Zivaka.[26]

"My good Zivaka, take this spade and seek around about Takshila on every side and whatever plant you see which is not medicinal bring it to me. During this period Zivaka examined all the plants of the area thoroughly and minutely but found all of them containing one or other medicinal value. At the end of seven days period when Zivaka returned to his teacher with the answer that he had not come across any plant with no medicinal value, the teacher felt satisfied that his student Zivaka has the requisite knowledge and declared him to have completed his education of medical science and permitted him to return home."

From this example it transpires that the teacher would give test to his students to judge the knowledge though not in every case. What is clear from the example is that the teacher would permit the student to return home to practise the science or technology only when he was satisfied that the student concerned was competent to enter into the profession and was competent to practise the same. In so far as other disciplines and trades are concerned there was no regular system of conducting terminal examination. Under the apprentice system of technical education where a student was given training as an apprentice with a master technician, the period of training was stipulated in advance. However, when the teacher found the apprentice not upto the mark on expiry of the period, a further extension was given to complete the training to enable the student to thoroughly learn the technique of trade.

Under the Ashram system of education where the education in Dhanur Veda and military science and other certain disciplines was imparted, there are only scattered references of giving a terminal examination to the students to mark the completion of the training. However, there are evidences in *Mahabharaea* to suggest the imaginative methods of testing and ranking a student with regard to his proficiency in that skill were some time followed.

Guru Drona was appointed as teacher for the Pandav and Kuru Princes in the technology of Dharmveda which includes archery, bow etc. At the end of the learning, the Guru Drona with a view of ranking the princes gave a test to them, which consisted of hitting the left eye of a bird planted on a tree.

In the context of above, it will be seen that terminal examination in technical education was not the essential feature not there was any relevance under the domestic system of ancient India. However, whenever a test was given to a student that would be of a very imaginative kind unlike the monotonous type of question papers as set under the modern system of examination.

REFERENCES

1. Ancient Indian History & Civilization' by Mazumdai, p.550.

2. 'Fine Art' by V.A. Smith.

2(a) Ancient Indian Education, p. 74 by F.E. Keay

3. The Indian Craftsman
A.K. Coomaraswamy, Ch. vi.
Mediacal Sinhalese Art, A.K. Coomaswamy p.63

3(a) Rig Veda ix-112

4. Rig Veda iv-179

5. Rig Veda i, 110, 3
Rig Veda i,111, 1

6. स होवाचर्ग्वदं भगवोऽध्योमि, यजुर्वेदं, सामवेदमाथर्वणं चतुर्थम्, इतिहासपुराणं पञ्चमं वेदानां वेंद, पित्र्यं, राशिं, दैवं, निधिं, वाकोवाक्यमेकायंन, देवविद्यां, ब्रह्मविद्यां, भूतविद्यां, क्षत्रविद्यां, नक्षत्रविद्यां, सर्पदेवजनविद्याम्, एतद्भगवोऽध्येमि॥2॥

7. जनको ह् वैदेहो बहुदक्षिणेन यज्ञेनेजे। तत्र ह् कुरूपञ्चालानां ब्राह्मणा अभिसमेता बभूवुस्तस्य ह जनकस्य वैदेहस्य विजिज्ञासा बभूव, कः खिदेषां ब्राह्मणानामनूचानतम इति। स ह गवां सहस्त्रमवरूरोध, दश दश पादा एकैकस्याः श्रृंङ्ग्योराबद्धा बभूवुः॥1॥

8 (i) Kautilya Ka Arthshastra, pp. 100-102. by Gairola V.
(ii) Ibid., p. 105.
(iii) Age of Nandas and Mauryas p. 337. by N.K. Shastry

8(a) Mahabharta - 11C.

9. तालिमिव्यानि यदं ते ददाम्यत्राणि सर्वशः।
दण्डचक्रं महद् दिव्यं तब दास्यामि राघव ॥4॥
धर्मचक्रं ततो वीर फालचक्रं तथैव च।
विष्णुचक्रं तथात्युग्रमैन्द्रं चक्रं तथैव च ॥5॥
(श्री मद्रामायणे) सप्तविशः सर्गः

10. महप्वक्षिण काकुत्स्य रथोऽयं विजयाय ते।
दनस्तत महासत्त्व श्रीमञ्शत्रुनिवर्हण॥14॥
आरूहोयं रथं वीर राक्षसं जहि रावणम्।
मया सारथिना देव महेन्द्र इव दानवान् ॥16॥
Ramayana of Valmiki, pp. 1375, Yuddh Kanda

11. (अयोध्या काण्डे ज्यशीतितमः सर्गः)
Ramayuana of Valmiki, p.417. (Grifth Translation)

12. Chulluvagga, i. 27

12(a). Narada, "तत्र कर्म च यत् कुर्यादाचार्यस्यैव तत् फलम्"।

13. Manu Smriti, X-81-82.

14. Law Book of Narada.
See "Ancient Indian Education', pp. 349

15. The Industrial Art of India by Bird Wood, p. 142.
The Indian Craftsman by Coomarswamy Ch. VI.

16. Hinduism and Economic Growth, p. 18 by Vikas Mishra.

17. Also see Kautilya's Arthasastra IV. 1

18. Kali Das Ka Bharat, Pt. II, by B.S. Upadhaya

19. Civilization of Ancient India p. 132 (Renou Louis)

20. Jataka No. 487

21. Jataka No. 35, 171

Jataka No. 219

Jataka No. 200

Jataka No. 510, 415

22. See Anclent Indian Education by R.K. Mukerji

23. अपेतक्लमसंतापाः सुभिक्षाः सुप्रतिथयाः।
अपि प्रेष्यानुपादाय सर्वे स्म सुसुखोपिताः ॥6॥
(श्री मद् बाल्मीकीय रामायेण पुष्टे 426) (गीता प्रेस)

24. समावागणितान वासान् सप्ताष्टौ रघुनन्दनः।
बाल्मीकाथममागत्य वासं चक्रे महायशाः॥3॥
(उत्तरकाण्डे एक सप्ततितमः सर्गः)
(श्रीमद् बाल्मीकीय रामायणे)

25. सर्वे ज्ञानोपसम्पन्नाः सर्वे समुदिता गुणैः।
तैगमपि महातेजा रामः सत्यपराक्रमः ॥26॥
इष्टः सर्वस्य लोकस्य शशाङ्क इव निर्मलः।
गजस्कन्धेऽश्वपृष्ठे च रथचर्यासु सम्मतः॥27॥
धनुर्वेदे च निरतः पितुः शुश्रूपणे रतः।
ते चापि मनुजव्यामा वैदिकाध्ययने रताः ॥36॥
पितृशुथूपणरता धनुर्वेदे च निष्ठिताः।

26. Chullauagga, VIII, 1, 4.

9

The EPIC Period

9

THE EPIC PERIOD

The Epic Period which is echoed with the kathas of *Ramoyana* and *Mahabharata* and the heroic deeds of Lord Rama and Lord Krishna and of the fiercest war of Pandavas and Kaurvas is one of the important period of ancient India. In fact, the great Hindu religion is so deeply influenced by the charismatic life of Lord Rama and Lord Krishna that the majority of festivals of the Hindus - Deewali, Dussehra, etc. are all linked with the significant events of the life of these two divinities who are regarded incarnation of Lord Vishnu. It is perhaps difficult to pin point the year and age of *Ramayana* and *Mahabharata.* However, the ancient Indian *Historians* generally opine these events to have taken place between 1000 B.C. to 800 B.C.[1] It is unfortunate that unnecessary controversies are raised some time to dispute the historicity of the material contained in them. As rightly commented by Dr. K.M. Munshi in his work *"Indian Inheritence". "No poet could evolve out of his own imagination, a picture at once so colossal, so vivid, so consistent in every detail. No number of poets could do it without stumbling into total incompatibilities either of fact or of view such as we find depicting the Mahabharata."*

It is worth while to mention that the Aryan Civilization was at its zoom in this period. The Varna-Ashram system i.e. classification according to caste and division of life span into four stages viz. Brahmcharya, Grihstha, Vanprastha and Sanyasa were observed scrupulously.

Shri Rama is still regarded as an ideal king and his reign is called as 'Ram Rajya' which was adopted by Gandhij. as the goal of independent India, is memorable in ancient Indian History being reckoned as the most ideal one. Besides the Aryan civilization, it appears there were two more civilizations existing in those days:

1. Vanar Civilization
2. Rakshasa Civilization

King Sugriva, Bali, Angada and Shri Hanuman belonged to Vanar Civilization. Ravana, Meghnad and Vibbishana, etc. were the stalwarts of Rakshasa Civilization.

As regards the education, the great epics of *Ramayana* and *Mahabharata* are full of mention of Ashramas of Rishis and Munies[2] and even Asuras. It was the common practice in those days that the Princes were sent to ashramas of gurus for receiving education not only relating to 'shastra' and scriptures but for armoury training also. It appears that for military training no separate ashramas were in vogue. Ashramas were normally manned by Brahmanas. The royal families were having their own Purohit and Priest or Kulguru who was responsible for performing all rituals and advise the king on all religious matters.

EDUCATION IN EPIC

From the evidence furnished by *Ramayana* and *Mahabharata,* it transpires that the education facilities in many disciplines of study were available besides in Vedas and Vedangas. The educational attainments of Shri Rama and his three brothers at the age of 16 have been described as under by the great Rishi Valmiki.[3]

"Versed in Vedas and still engaged in Vaidika studies, possessed of wide knowledge well grounded in the science of arms, hunting on horse back with bows and arrows,

expert in riding elephants, horses and war chariots, spirited heroic, already famous and looking far ahead of all virtues."

Similarly Shri Hanuman who was in the dress of Bhiku, when met Shri Rama and Lakshmana wandering in forests in search of Sita, the following assessment of educational attainment of Shri Hanuman who belonged to 'Vanar Civilization' was made by Shri Rama:[4]

"He is 'Vakyakusla' i.e. knew the science of words (Grammar Etymology, etc.) as well as the art of using words (Rhetorics, etc.). He must have been trained in or moulded by studies in the Rig Veda, have retained or memorized the Yajur Veda and acquired skill in the Sam Veda and he must have learnt (Srutam) in many ways the whole science of Vyakarna (Grammar philology, Etymology and phonetics). He was in fact an ideal counsellor for a king."

This all shows that besides the Aryan civilization the Vanar civilization was also sufficiently developed in regard to education and was also based upon Vedic study. -

INSTITUTIONS OF EDUCATION

1. Ashramas

The most common institutions of education in those days were hermitages of Acharyas, Munies, Kulgurus, etc. Some of the hermitages which were called Ashramas were very big and spacious. Ashrama of Muni Bhardwaj[5] where Bharta while meeting his elder brother Shri Rama in forest stayed in way along with his army has been described to have separate Saya/guest house, arrangement of music and dancing girls, stalls to accommodate elephant and horses besides the facility of meditation and education in various disciplines. The Ashrama of Valmiki and sage Vasishta must also be very capacious with facilities of education in Vedas, Upvedas and Military art, etc.

As regards the details of disciplines of study in these Ashramas, the hermitage of Rishi Kanwa deserves mention. There were specialists in each of the four Vedas, Kalpasastra, Theology metrics, Grammar and Nirukta. Similarly, specialists in Philosophy and in physical science and art including the experts of constructing sacrificial altars, experts having knowledge of material sciences and Zoology have also been mentioned.

In the Ashrama of Valmiki 'Dhanur Veda' and also other disciplines of military training were imparted to Lov and Kush (twin sons of Shri Rama) by sage Valmiki. Similarly there is mention of many other hermitages and ashramas in *Ramayana* and *Mahabharata.*

2. Courts of Learned Kings

The other institutions of learning were the court of kings where learned gatherings were held by the king inviting scholars from all corners in the tournaments and debates and various controversies were discussed and sorted out. The court of King Janaka has been mentioned one such place.

FATHER OR GRAND-FATHER AS TEACHER[6]

From the evidence in Mahabharata it appears that it was not compulsory for the boy to go to the ashrama of Rishi and Acharya for education. In case where father or grand father or an elderly man in the family was available well versed in various disciplines of study relevant to his profession and caste, he would act as teacher of their sons or grandsons, etc. This is corroborated by several instances in Mahabharata, one mentioning that Dhritrashtra, Pandu princes and Vidhura, underwent studentship of Bhishma who imparted them education not only in Nitishastra, Etihasa and Puranas and truth of Veda and Vedangas but also the military training in Dhanurveda, wielding of swords and shields, etc. Similarly Arjuna acted as teachcr of his son Abhimanyu and other princes.

ADMISSION INTO STUDENTSHIP

It was the usual practice that the aspiring student would approach the teacher of repute for admission into studentship who in turn would examine the student with reference to his birth, mental calibre and character before accepting him as his disciple. No knowledge could be imparted much less of Vedas unless one has formally become a disciple. The admission was open to the three - twice born castes, only. Howevcr, all the four castes were eligible for the Vedic recitation[7].

One who had enrolled himself as a disciple or a student would be governed by the following rules:

(i) He should perform all acts as desired by his preceptor at all costs by body, mind and speech.
(ii) He should study sitting at the feet of his preceptor with keenness to learn.
(iii) He should follow his preceptor and should eat, should think, should sit down after his preceptor has done so. He should rise from bed before the preceptor rises and should sleep after the preceptor has gone to his bed.
(iv) He should spend one fourth of his life as Brahamacharin and should give the preceptor his fee and return home with his permission only and become a house holder.

DISCIPLINES OF STUDY

As per evidence of epic, the period of study was fixed for the students and there was no terminal examination. The teacher would guide the students with regard to study. It transpires from the study of epic thoughts that while studentship was the first stage of life of every member of the twice born class, the course of study was not uniform for all the classes and varied depending upon the duties prescribed for each class. The Brahmans were expected to be engaged in teaching and performing religious ceremonies and rites for others and be proficient in Vedas. The Kshatriyas were enjoined with the duties of defence and protection of the country and of its people. Vaisyas were expected to engage themselves in agriculture, accounts, commerce, trade, etc. The education imparted to all these three classes, must, therefore, had two stages. At the first stage curriculum common to all the three classes, was covered by the teacher, while the second stage comprised of the special education relevant to the occupation—one is supposed to pursue after the study. A Brahman must be proficient in Vedas and other Scriptures and also the religious practices being followed at different occasions. Similarly, Kshatriya must learn Dhanurveda (Archery), club fights, swords and driving of elephants, etc.

Several references in *Mahabhara:a* also show that besides the above disciplines of study sixty four kalas i.e. Arts and Crafts were taught and were in practice.

Similarly in *Ramayana* craftsmen in various skills have been mentioned[8], which suggests that facilities of training in various vocations and crafts were available in that period.

EXAMINATION METHODS IN EPIC PERIOD

The study of *Mahabharata* shows the imaginative methods followed in those days for testing excellence and knowledge of students, especially in military science which was included under the general term of 'Dhanurveda' means Archery and was perfected by the Princes and Kings.

Drona was appointed as a teacher to teach Dhanurveda to Pandu and Kuru Princes and they became well versed to the use of all kinds of weapons including the Archery. A test was conducted for them to put their knowledge to test which comprised of fixing an artificial bird with Two eye symbols on a branch of tree and all princes were one by one asked to hit the target—the left eye of the bird. Every prince attempted it. However, before launching the arrow and after a student had taken position to just hit, Guru the teacher put them a question "What are you seeing?" Now each of them replies it in a different way, some mentioned the branch and leaves, the other would mention of astray thoughts cropping up his mind at the time and yet another would name the bird itself. The Guru was disappointed, asked each of them to abandon the effort. Last came Arjun, the same question was put to him also and the reply came that he was not seeing anything but the ball of the left eye of the bird which was to be hitted by the arrow. In fact, that was the exact reply and perfect position which a warrior should have before launching an arrow, that he should only see the exact target not any other thing and not any other thought in his mind. The Guru was satisfied and asked Arjun to hit the bird and the next moment the bird was on the ground with the arrow piercing through the ball of its eye.

Yet, another method adopted by the Guru Drona who tested the knowledge of Kuru and Pandu Princes finds mention in *Mahabharata,* All the Princes were taken to the river side accompanied by Drona who desired that he should take bath in the river and went dccp inside thc water and took a dip therein. An artificial man eater fish jump upon thc Guru to swallow him and the Guru raised alarm to save his life. All thc Princes were at their wits end as what to do. While Arjuna showed thc alertness of his mind and brought his bow (Dhanu) and hit the Crocodilc by an arrow in such a remarkablc manner that the jaw of the crocodilc would remain open with the arrow in between not allowing the crocodilc to close it to swallow his Guru. This was a test of precision of hitting thc target given by the Guru which was an essential requirement to bccomt an excellent and expert Dhanurdhar.

We also come across the story of Eklavya—an ambitious and aspirant youth of Bhil tribe who approached Drona to enrol him as his pupil However, Drona declined the request as he would teach only the Princes for which he had been appointed by Bhishma. Eklavya was disheartened and returned home, however, took a vow that he must be an recellent Dhanurdhar expert in Dhanurveda and would choose none but Drona as his Guru. He commissioned a clay statue of Drona and practised the art of archery with an abiding faith in his Guru Drona and made determination to becomc Dhanurdhar and perfect the art of Archery When Drona as a coincidence passed from that way and saw him practising the art of Archery with his statue standing side by, got surprised and gave him a test asking him to show knowledge and expertise in Dhanurvidya on a barking dog. Eklavya being perfect in the art hits across the jaw of the dog, stitching both the jaws with arrow, bringing the dog to silence.

Similar other evidences are there to indicate that novel methods were adopted by the teachers to test the knowledge of their students and so on.

It may, however, be mentioned that neither it was the universal practice to give terminal test to every student nor it was necessary to do so by the teacher who was fully and wholly responsible for equipping his student with the skill and knowledge at the command of the teacher in that science or art.

REFERENCES

1. Ancient Indian Education, p. 18. by F.E. Keay

   Professor Robert Philip Goldman, University of California.

2. Mahabbaria, i. 70
   Ibid., IX, 42
   Ramayana, VI. 126

3. सर्वे ज्ञानोपसम्पन्ना: सर्वे समुदिता गुणै:।
   तेपामपि महातेजा राम: सत्यपराक्रम:।।26।।
   इष्ट: सर्वस्य लोकस्य शशाङ्क इव निर्मल:।
   गजस्कन्धेऽश्वपृष्ठे च रथचर्यासु सम्मत:।।27।।
   धनुर्वेदे च निरत: पितु: शुश्रूपणे रत:। (बालकाण्डे अष्टादशसर्ग:),
   (श्रीमद् बाल्मीकीय रामायणे)

4. नूनं व्याकरणं कृत्त्रममन बहुधा सुतम्।
   बहु व्याहरतानेन न किचिंद्पशब्दितम्।।29।।
   ते चापि मनुज वैदिकाध्ययने रता:।।36।।
   पितृशुश्रपणरता धनुर्वेदे च निष्ठिता:।
   नानृग्वेदविनीतस्य नायजुर्वेदधारिण:।
   नासामवेदविदुष: शक्यमेवं विभाषितुम्।।28।।
   (किष्किन्धा काण्डे तृतीय सर्ग:)

5. अपेतणमसंतापा सुभिक्षा: सुप्रतिश्रया:।
   अपि प्रेष्यानुपादाय सर्वे स्म सुसुखोपिता:।।6।।
   सेवकोसहित हम सब लोग ग्लानि और संताप से रहित
   इति पादातयोधाश्च हत्त्य श्र्वारोहबन्धका:।
   अनाथास्तं विधिं लब्ध्वा वाचमेतामुदीरयन्।।60।।

   (श्रीमद् बाल्मीकीय रामायेण अयोध्या काण्डे)

6. **Mahabharta, i. 223.**

7. **Mahabharta, XII, 327.**

8. मणिकराश्च ये केचित् कुम्भकराश्च शोभना:।
सूत्रकर्मधिशेषज्ञा चे च शस्त्रोपजीविन:॥12॥

मायूरका: काकचिका वेधका रोचकास्तथा।
दन्तकारा: सुधाकारा ये च गन्धोपजीविन:॥13॥

सुवर्णकारा: प्रख्यातास्तथा कम्बलकारका:।
स्नापकोष्णोदका वैद्या धूपका: शोण्डिकास्तथा॥14॥

रजकास्तुन्नवाशाश्य ग्रामघोषमहत्तरा:।
शैलूणश्च सह स्त्रीभिर्यान्ति कैवर्तकास्तथा॥15॥

समाहिता वेदविदो ब्राह्मणा वृत्तसम्मता:।
गोरथैर्भरतं यान्तमनुजग्मु: सहस्त्रश:॥16॥

(अयोध्या काण्डेत्रयशीतितम: सर्ग:)

10

Buddhist Education and Evaluation System

10

BUDDHIST EDUCATION AND EVALUATION SYSTEM

The Era of Buddhist education dominated the Indian scene for several centuries when monasteries—the churches of Buddhism sprang up in every corner and length and breadth of the country. Gautum—the Buddha was born some where in 567 B.C. and obtained his Nirvan in 487 B.C. at an advanced age of eighty. However, Buddhism had been in vogue in India for more than a thousand years. The main theme of Buddhism is characterized by a broad spirit of philanthropy and pursuing 'Madhyam Marg' (middle path) avoiding the two extremities. It differs from the Hindu philosophy in the following aspects:

(i) Non-recognition of Vedas

(ii) Non-recognition of Brahmanism

(iii) Proclamation of equality in respect of castes. In fact this was the main spring-board of Buddhism. The pretentions regarding arbitrary distinction of castes were scattered to wind by the strong logic of the great Buddha.

A Monastry at Orissa

The scripture of Buddhism providing guidance to its devotees took its final shape after one or two centuries of Buddha's death and is known as Tripitaka. It comprises of three volumes:

1. *Vinaya-Pitaka*

This lays down a body of rules and regulations for the guidance of its devotees and is considered to be most important.

2. *Suta-Pitaka*

This is also a very important work and is a collection of religious discoveries of Buddha.

3. *Abhi-Dharam Pitaka*

It means higher religion and has been written in the form of question and answer. However the subject matter is the same as dealt with in SutaPitaka. The Vinaya-Pitaka has the following parts:

(i) Sutta Vibhanga
(ii) Khandhakas
(iii) Parivala

(i) The Sutta Vibhanga contains a list of various offences 227 in number which a Buddhist monk should avoid. The list of offences is recited publicly in an assembly of monks at each monastry twice a month and at the end every monk is supposed to divulge his offence or default, if any, and punishment is imposed upon him as per the rules.

(ii) *Khandhakas:* They contain the rules and regulations on different ceremonies of daily life of a monk. The act of admission of a novice, the rules of robes, dress, meal and clothing, etc. Khandhakas has two sections:

(a) Mahavagga
(b) Chullavegga

The rules are supposed to have been laid down by the Buddha himself.

(iii) *Parivala:* This is a resume of the first two books.

BUDDHIST EDUCATION

One of the characteristic features of Buddhist education was that the latter has not based upon Vedic Study or recitation or tapas or yogas. Also it did not recognize Brahmanic hierarchy. The teachers were not essentially Brahman. The admission to the Buddhist community or Buddhist education was open to all without any discrimination of caste.

INSTITUTIONS OF' LEARNING

Viharas orMonasteries formed the learning point of Buddhist education. These Monasteries were in fact regarded as Church of Buddhism where the Buddhist monks or the community called as 'Sangha' settled down for all purpose, and were reckoned as the order of Buddhism.

ADMISSION TO BUDDHIST EDUCATION

In order to receive Buddhist education the novice had to approach the Buddhist monk who was a full member of the order as Acharya or preceptor. The novice would regard his Acharya or Upajjhaya as his father and in turn the latter would regard the pupil as his son. It was perscribed by Buddha that the two united by mutual reverence, confidence and communion of life should reach a high stage in the order.

There were two stages of admission—provisional admission and final admission. The admission to Sangha was open for all without any consideration of caste. However, one should be of minimum 8 years of age and should not be slave or debtor nor in the service of the King. He should also not be suffering from certain diseases and should obtain the consent or permission of his parent. The act of admission to the order of Buddhism consisted of cutting off hair and beard by the aspirant and put on yellow robe adjusting to cover one shoulder only. He should sit down squatting in the feet of his preceptor and salute the Bhikkus with his head uttering the sacred 'Sutra'.

I take refuge in the Buddha[1]
I take refuge in the Dhamma.
I take refuge in the Sangha.

And this completes the admission ceremony. The candidate was called as novice.

FINAL ADMISSION ON UPSAMPDA

For the final admission which was named as Upsampda one should be minimum of twenty years of age and should have desire of full admission into the order. The other conditions were similar to that of the provisional admission. It is, however, implied that he should have shown satisfactory conduct or progress during the period of provisional admission.

Alter the admission in the order whether provisional admission or full admission the pupil or novice was subjected to strict rules governing to his conduct, robes, eating and living and observing of discipline. He was supposed to lead the life of strenuous morality, under the guidance and supervision of his preceptor.

The pupil was expected to show respect to his teacher and superiors, he was given Alm-Bowl and robe and other simple things. Begging for food And subsistence was almost compulsory. However, invitation from wealthy person for food at their houses occasionally was permitted. The senior monks were also supposed to put themselves into meditation which was in fact considered important for spiritual progress. Even at the time of Fa-hien—theChinese traveller—this was continuing. An extract from his travelling reads as under:

"The regular business of monks was to perform acts of meritorious virtue and to recite sutras and sit rapt in meditation."

CURRICULUM OF BUDDHIST EDUCATION

I-T.- Siang-a Chinese traveller who came to India and was here from 673-687 A.D. furnishes a vivid picture of Buddhist education which was being imparted in those days in the monastries. According to him an extensive study of Sanskrit grammar which served as the foundation course leading to mets a - physics and philosophy was done. The method of teaching was mainly oral.[2] There is ample evidence to show that he common practice in those days was, learning every thing by rot method. Teaching through discussion and debate was also prevalent and utmost importance was given to this skill. Vinay which is considered as a Bible of Buddhism and other texts i.e. 'Tripitaka' were studied, Buddhism regarded the body health of a person as an important aspect to enable him to improve his religious merit and spiritual condition. As such medicine formed an important subject of specialized study. At Taxila University there was an exclusive school for medicine. Here a noted physician named Zivaka received his medical education and performed very difficult operation thereafter. Similarly Charka a pioneer authority of Ayurvedic medicine was given a royal place by Buddhist king Kanishka.

ASSESSMENT AND EVALUATION

A deep insight into Buddhism and the system of imparting instructions to its pupil gives an idea that the following practices and methods of evaluation were in vogue:

(i) Assessment by the teacher
(ii) Self assessment
(iii) Valuation by the general assembly

(i) Evaluation by the Teacher

In Buddhist system the education comprised of religious instructions and of general conduct. It was essential for the student called novice to put himself under the pupilage of his teacher who was supposed to exercise close supervision.

An extract from I.T. Siang description read as under:[3] *"He (teacher) inspects pupil's moral conduct and warns him of defects and transgressions, whenever he finds his pupil faulty, he makes him seek remedies and repent."*

Though there is no specific mention regarding the educational performance of the student, however, it is well implied that similar procedure must have been followed by the teacher, whenever he would have found his students not showing progress in respect of memorising the religious literature which was given by the teacher. There is no evidence to show that a student had at any time faced expulsion from the order on this account.

(ii) Self Assessment System

This was a unique system being followed under Buddhist order. As per the system the rule book of Buddhism called Sutta-Vibhanga which contains a list of different kinds of offences in respect of the conduct including education of monk was recited every mean and full moon day before the gathering of monks and nuns. At the end of description of each class of offences the questions were put to the assembled monks whether they were pure with regard to it and anyone who felt that he had committed violation in any aspect would speak and was supposed to have confessed it and a penance was imposed upon him according to the gravity of his offence.

This can be very well treated as Self Assessment System in respect of the moral conduct which was the part and parcel of Buddhist system of education.

(iii) Evaluation by General Assembly

I. T. Siang, the Chinese traveller who was in India during seventh century mentions regarding education in the monastries as under:

"A place was also given to discussions and debate, at least in the higher part of the course and the man's ability seems to have been very largely judged by his power to vanquish opponents in discussion. These were such men apparently who got royal appointments and whose names were as a reward, inscribed in lofty gates."'

It is implied that the performance of a student in respect of his skill in discussion and debate was evaluated by the assembly of people through consensus voice though the final judgment was given by the King if such discussions were held in his court) or the learned men who occupied front seats in the assembly.

SIGNIFICANT ROLE OF BUDDHIST EDUCATION

An outstanding contribution of the Buddhist education as has been marked in the ancient history, lies in the fact that the monastries—Viharas which were the church of Buddhism assumed a significant role of a good centre of learning. Some of the monastries possessed such a grandeur in term of their beautiful buildings, library and other infrastructure of academics that they have been well compared with the modern Universities and in no term less in academic excellence. These Universities prominent being Nalanda University were so famed that these attracted scholars and students not only from every corner of India but from other countries also. No less significant is the fact that the novel methods which these ancient seats of learning introduced were really imaginative one and can be well termed as the beginning of the modern concept of examination. The 'Pandita' system of entrance test followed by the Nalanda University. Vikramshila and 'Shalaka' method of examination introduced by Mithila University have important place. Though Buddhism as a religion is almost extinct in India, but in neighbouring countries such as Cylon, China, Tibet, Thailand, Burma, etc. the majority of population is still follower of this great religion which has its deep root in Hinduism.

REFERENCES

1. Mahavagga, i. 38.
   * Fa-Hien (Leggis Translation) p. 44.
2. I. T-Siang, p. 183.
3. I. T-Siang, p. 120.
   (Takakusu's ed.)
4. I.T.- Siang p. 183.